KEEPING THE PROMISE?

Keeping the Promise?

The Debate Over Charter Schools

EDITED BY
Leigh Dingerson
Barbara Miner
Bob Peterson
Stephanie Walters

A Rethinking Schools Publication
in collaboration with The Center for Community Change

Keeping the Promise?
The Debate Over Charter Schools
Edited by Leigh Dingerson, Barbara Miner, Bob Peterson, and Stephanie Walters

A Rethinking Schools Publication
in collaboration with The Center for Community Change.

Rethinking Schools, Ltd., is a nonprofit educational publisher of books, booklets, and a quarterly journal on school reform, with a focus on issues of equity and social justice. To request additional copies of this book or a catalog of other publications, or to subscribe to the quarterly journal *Rethinking Schools*, contact:

Rethinking Schools
1001 East Keefe Avenue
Milwaukee, Wisconsin 53212 USA
800-669-4192
www.rethinkingschools.org

© 2008 Rethinking Schools, Ltd.
First edition

Cover Design: Patrick Flynn
Book Design: Kate Hawley
Proofreading: Jennifer Morales
Production Manager: Barbara Miner
Business Manager: Mike Trokan

Special thanks to the Open Society Institute
for its generous support of this project.

ISBN: 978-0-942961-38-6

Dream Dust

By Langston Hughes

Gather out of star-dust
    Earth-dust,
    Cloud-dust,
    Storm-dust,
And splinters of hail,
One handful of dream-dust
    Not for sale.

Table of Contents

Preface

Keeping the Promise? The Debate Over Charter Schools grows out of five "white papers" commissioned by the Open Society Institute.

The papers were presented by their authors at a forum, "Charter Schools: Keeping the Promise or Dismantling Communities?" at the Center for Community Change in Washington, D.C., on March 28, 2007, cosponsored by the Center, the Open Society Institute, and the Forum for Education and Democracy.

The event was moderated by Dr. Linda Darling-Hammond, who later agreed to write a sixth white paper on the policy implications of the charter movement. That paper is included here as the seventh chapter.

The Center for Community Change asked Rethinking Schools to publish the white papers, in order to continue and deepen the discussion on the role of charter schools in the United States. The Center and Rethinking Schools then set up a joint editorial team for the book, including Leigh Dingerson from the Center and Stephanie Walters and Bob Peterson from Rethinking Schools. Barbara Miner, a former managing editor of *Rethinking Schools*, agreed to coordinate and help edit the book. As the project unfolded, the editors decided to add an additional chapter to explore the lessons offered by several charters that, in distinct ways, are attempting to "keep the promise" of the progressive educators who helped develop the charter school concept. The sixth chapter, which presents the stories of these schools, was not one of the originally commissioned white papers.

Rethinking Schools is pleased to be able to present the white papers to a broader audience. We are grateful to the Open Society Institute—a private operating and grantmaking foundation that works to build vibrant and tolerant democracies whose governments are accountable to its citizens—for its decision to commission the original white papers, and for its generous support toward the publication of this collection.

We also would like to thank the writers for their original papers and subsequent revisions.

As with any diverse collection of essays on a controversial topic, the publication of these papers does not imply organizational endorsement of the ideas contained within, nor does it imply that all authors agree with the various perspectives. We hope that the essays will engender substantive and ongoing discussion about how best to bring quality education to all students, in line with the broader goal of forging a multiracial democracy.

Bob Peterson
for Rethinking Schools
www.rethinkingschools.org
March 2008

Introduction

In the last two decades, charter schools have emerged as one of the dominant reforms in public education in the United States. While desegregation and magnet schools were hallmarks of education reform in the 1970s and into the 1980s, by the end of the century charter schools had eclipsed such initiatives to take center stage.

From only a handful of schools in the early 1990s, by the 2006–07 school year there were more than 4,000 charter schools enrolling more than a million students in 40 states and the District of Columbia. In some urban districts, charters enrolled a growing percentage of public school students—as much as 57 percent in New Orleans and 27 percent in Dayton, Ohio, and Washington, D.C. The for-profit Edison Schools, meanwhile, had 157 schools, dwarfing the size of many urban districts.

The charter school movement has roots in a progressive agenda that, as educator Joe Nathan wrote in *Rethinking Schools* in 1996, viewed charters as "an important opportunity for educators to fulfill their dreams, to empower the powerless, and to help encourage a bureaucratic system to be more responsive and more effective."

Early proponents of charter schools did not view their reform as a cure-all but as one of many vehicles to improve public schools, particularly in urban areas where this country's dichotomies of race and class are most pronounced. As Lisa Stulberg and the late Eric Rofes wrote in their 2004 book *The Emancipatory Promise of Charter Schools*, charters are one specific reform initiative that can "begin to open up a wider discussion of a new, progressive vision for public education."

Unfortunately, the charter concept also appealed to conservatives wedded to a free-market, privatization agenda. And it is they who, over the past decade, have taken advantage of the conservative domination of national politics to seize the upper hand in the charter school movement.

The question today is, where is the charter school concept heading? Will it help spur reform so that all public schools, charter and traditional, can live up to the promise of a quality education for all and serve the needs of an increasingly multiracial democracy? Or will the movement drain away necessary resources and energy from districtwide reform and instead promote a system of individual consumer choice, inevitably coupled with all the inequalities inherent in a market system of distribution?

This country is on the cusp of a new political dialogue. The conservative stranglehold on political debate is ending, opening up opportunities for progressives to regain the initiative. How this opening will affect public education in general and charter schools in particular is not yet clear, but it ushers in possibilities not imaginable a decade ago.

Evaluating the charter school reform movement presents several distinct challenges. First, despite its reliance on free-market principles, it is a multifaceted movement and must be analyzed as such. Second, it highlights inherent problems with the concept of public school "choice," especially in urban areas where semiprivate charter franchises are increasingly dominant. Third, it raises the issue of overly bureaucratic systems and rules. Finally, there are broader matters facing not just charters but all schools, in particular the need for quality teachers and systemwide reform, and the relationship of public schools to broader issues of social justice and democracy.

Within that context, we offer this collection of essays to promote dialogue on how the charter school movement can fulfill its progressive potential and, as Ted Sizer and George Wood argue in their opening essay, promote values of equity, access, public purpose, and public ownership that are essential to all public schools.

A Multifaceted Movement

It is impossible to lump together our country's public schools: well-funded schools in privileged suburbs are far different than under-resourced schools in poor urban neighborhoods. Likewise, charter schools come in many varieties: they are shaped by a state's charter school laws, by the motivations and capabilities of the charter school's founders, and by the broader local, state, and national political climate.

That being said, several legal requirements are common to all charter schools. They are publicly funded, are nonreligious, are not to charge tuition, and must obey civil rights regulations.

Some charter schools have strong ties to their community, are led by experienced educators, and are committed to providing all children a comprehensive education that meets their needs. Others are led by entrepreneurs, sometimes as part of a national franchise, who too often see schools primarily as a source of money and profits and whose educational experience is limited. Many charter schools fall somewhere between these two poles.

Philosophically, the charter school movement started with several core assumptions. Two are most important: first, that freedom from bureaucratic rules and union contracts will foster innovation and improve academic achievement; and, second, that the lessons from the charter movement's successes will be used to improve public education overall. Any discussion of charter schools must ask not only whether charters promote a worthwhile vision of public education, but also whether they are faithful to their own promises.

The essays in this book tell a story of what could be, but also what should not be. As the Ohio experience shows, too often charter schools have been used by free-market ideologues for political and financial gain. At the same time, schools such as The Next Step/El Proximo Paso in Washington, D.C., are using the charter model to reinvigorate ties with the community and to promote an education that meets the needs of its students. Clearly, the future of the charter school movement is still unfolding.

The Many Meanings of Choice

While academic excellence and equity of access were dominant themes in education following the Civil Rights Movement, the concept of "choice" has risen to new heights in recent decades. A fluid and problematic concept, it nonetheless strikes home with many Americans; used properly and in moderation, it can ensure that public education is sensitive to the varying needs of this country's 50 million public school students representing an escalating number of nationalities and languages.

White and middle-class families in the suburbs have made a choice of geography that provides them access to schools they generally like and support. For poor people in the cities, especially people of color, choices are more difficult. Thus it is not surprising that many urban families may see charters as a choice of a safer school, smaller classes, and more meaningful academics.

Virtually all segments of the charter school movement have targeted urban areas. Some hope to counteract inequity, spur innovation and better meet the needs of marginalized students. Others, taking advantage of the frustration that inevitably follows when districts are allowed to deteriorate, seek fame and fortune. Some hope to gain enough "market share" that they are on par, and compete, with traditional schools. Finally, there are those who view charters as a way to get rid of public schools altogether.

The elixir of an individualized bailout from a struggling system has serious side effects, however. It can create a painful wedge in many communities, especially among African-Americans; it can weaken the political will for a collective solution to the problems in public education; and it can promote the deterioration of traditional schools. As highly motivated and engaged families pull their children from traditional public schools, urban districts have fewer resources—both financial and human—to address their many problems. The worse the schools get, the more appealing the escape to charters and private schools, all of which feeds into the conservative dream of replacing public education with a free-market system of everyone for themselves, the common good be damned. Beleaguered urban districts, meanwhile, sometimes seem to give up on systemwide improvement and instead take a triage approach of abandoning some schools while providing "life boats," often in the form of small niche schools with a selective student body.

Too often, charter schools and "choice" public schools prefer, in practice if not in rhetoric, to educate "the deserving poor." There is far less inclination to serve students whose parents are absent or uninvolved, or who have severe physical or emotional educational needs, or who have run afoul of the juvenile justice system, or who don't speak English as their first language. Perhaps the most glaring example involves students with special education needs. Such students are increasingly overrepresented in traditional public schools, making a mockery of reforms that held out the promise that special ed students would not be treated as second-class citizens.

The essay on New Orleans underscores how that city's market-driven system of charters is based on the argument that choice creates healthy competition between schools. Yet, as the essay points out, there are devastating consequences for those who, by choice or by necessity, remain in the traditional public schools. The New Orleans story also underscores the inherent conflict between a strategy of "competition," where there must be winners and losers, and a strategy of equity where the successes of one sector are used to enhance the other.

For both charter and traditional public schools, the question is how to develop a system that recognizes individual preferences, but not by limiting the choices and opportunities available to others.

What is necessary is a commitment to serving all students, and to guard against the danger of linking choice with exclusion and privilege.

At the same time, progressives must guard against dismissing all alternatives to the traditional public school system. There are times when a focused commitment to the specific needs of specific students is both necessary and positive, or when one must break through the boundaries of traditional schooling in order to create a working model of what could be.

The Freedom Schools established by the Student Nonviolent Organizing Committee and other civil rights groups in 1964 are a well-known example of finding a vision of education outside of the public school system. Similarly, many "free schools" and "alternative schools" in the 1960s and 1970s were an important antidote to the dehumanizing factory model of education that valued standardization above all else. More recently, the Coalition of Essential Schools was founded in 1984 to promote equitable, intellectually vibrant, and personalized schools that, while operating within the boundaries of public education, oftentimes did so outside established district procedures. These examples show, in different ways, the power of individuals working together to create schools that challenge the inequities and inadequacies of too many traditional public schools.

The charter school movement does not grow directly out of such examples. But the involvement in charter schools of progressives with similar visions should not be dismissed.

At the same time, one cannot deny that the charter school concept, as a movement, has been hijacked by individuals, groups, and corporations who are guided by free-market principles, often with a hostility to unions, and who do not necessarily embrace core values of equity, access, public purpose, and public ownership.

If charter school reform is to live up to its initial promises, progressives must regain the initiative and use charter schools to empower teachers and parents, to challenge the dominant narrative in public education of standardization, selectivity, and privilege, and to use those lessons to improve all public schools.

Bureaucracy and Union Contracts

From the beginning, the most important and consistent themes of charter school proponents were that freedom from bureaucracy and from union contract provisions would spur innovation and achievement.

The claims, especially dissatisfaction with bureaucracy, struck a chord among families frustrated with how well public schools were serving their children's needs, especially when the claims were coupled with anecdotes of teachers and parents prevented from implementing worthwhile educational practices.

Without a doubt, too many public school districts suffer from rote thinking and top-down mandates that are codified into bureaucratic rules and regulations. Sadly, the juggernaut of standardized testing and drill-and-kill curriculum promoted by the federal No Child Left Behind act (NCLB) has only heightened the problem of harmful mandates.

As for union contracts, there is no doubt that some complaints are valid, especially concerns over rigid seniority rules that make it difficult for schools to hire a staff committed to a common vision.

But it would be naive to ignore that some of the antiunion rhetoric comes from conservatives wedded to an antiunion ideology. Some union rules are the result of hard-won protections—with civil rights, special education, academic freedom, and gender-based protections just a few examples. Other bureaucratic rules are designed to counteract problems of corruption or incompetence. And many union protections were fought for and won in order to safeguard the rights of teachers around issues such as due process, adequate pay, and decent working conditions—rights that every individual should have, and that have the added benefit of ensuring a stable corps of experienced teachers for our public schools.

The extent to which a charter school is exempt from the union contract or unnecessary bureaucracy varies, based not only on state legislation but the chartering organization's views and the ideology of a charter school's founders. The movement as a whole, however, remains committed to the view that bureaucracy and union agreements are to be circumvented whenever possible.

One of the biggest controversies surrounding the charter school movement is how well it has lived up to its promise of innovation and improved achievement as a result of its freedoms from bureaucracy and union agreements. Overall, studies have shown that charter schools perform either worse or just as well as comparable public schools, which leads to an unanswered question, as noted in the 2005 book *The Charter School Dust-Up*, by Martin Carnoy, Rebecca Jacobsen, Lawrence Mishel, and Richard Rothstein:

> "If, however, charter schools are not improving the achievement of disadvantaged children, it may be that the cause of low student performance is not bureaucratic rules but some-

thing else. When a treatment is based on a diagnosis, and the treatment doesn't work, it is prudent to examine not only whether the treatment should be improved, but also whether the diagnosis might be flawed."

Even if it is shown that certain bureaucratic rules, union requirements, or state and federal mandates stifle innovation and suffocate higher achievement, shouldn't they be thrown out or modified for all schools, not just charters?

Quality Teachers and Systemwide Reform

One of the problems facing many charter schools, and indeed public schools overall in urban and rural areas, is the insufficient number of excellent teachers committed to teaching all students. Studies have consistently shown that after socioeconomic status is taken into account, a good teacher is the single most important factor in student achievement.

Teacher certification for charter schools varies significantly by state. Some states require that charter schools hire certified teachers, some states such as Arizona and Texas do not, and some states set a percentage such as 25 percent or 50 percent certified teachers, according to the Education Commission of the States. Some require that charter school teachers be credentialed at the same level as other public schools only in college prep and core academic classes.

In its initial years, the charter school movement overall had a lower percentage than traditional public schools of certified teachers, and disproportionately relied on teachers with less experience. In fact, strong anecdotal evidence shows that many of the charter schools that have been favorites with the mainstream media have had an extraordinarily high percentage of new teachers and a high turnover rate.

Which raises an important question: is it possible to build a systemwide reform movement, as charter schools purport to be, if the movement can neither be sustained at a quality level nor replicated?

No one disputes that it is possible to build good schools, as individual charter, public, and private schools across the country demonstrate. The issue is creating a system of schools based on institutionalized structures and practices that ensure lasting success on a districtwide basis. Reforms are bound to fail if they rely on the voluntarism of idealistic, overworked teachers who burn out and leave the school once they decide to have a family or want any semblance of a meaningful personal life.

Such issues are related to questions of scale. Many good, experimental schools, both charter and traditional, rely on a particular vision that cannot be replicated on a significant basis without broader reforms such as adequate resources, a solid corps of qualified teachers, and a reinvigorated commitment to serving all children. In this context, perhaps it remains best to return to the original vision of charter schools as limited experiments designed to try out new ideas that can be used to improve education throughout the district.

Some in the charter school movement instead view charters as growing exponentially, becoming a substitute for traditional public schools. Yet when charters reach that tipping point where they become a significant sector unto themselves, immense problems arise—not just with maintaining quality, but also with undermining traditional public schools because those traditional schools have fewer resources and a higher percentage of disadvantaged students.

Finally, the larger the system of charter schools, the more glaring the need to address the issue of democratic control of our schools. In too many instances, important decisions are taken out of public control and ceded to boards of directors who have minimal public accountability beyond insuring against fraud and corruption. In the case of charter franchise operations, especially by for-profit companies, concerns of public accountability are especially pressing. For all their faults, school boards are democratically elected bodies that provide a mechanism for public input; for all their strengths, even nonprofit boards of directors do not have similar responsibilities to the public.

To date, there has been insufficient discussion of dealing with these complicated issues of scale, sustainability, replication, and public democratic control.

Unfettered free-market ideology, with its notion of proprietary ownership of any formula for success, has been especially harmful in undermining the original ideal that charter schools would champion innovation and share the lessons learned in order to improve all public schools. Too often, charter schools are far less innovative than promised and, when they do purport success, do not collaborate with other schools to share what works and, equally important, what doesn't work.

A Reinvigorated Commitment to All Children

Throughout the history of education in the United States, public schools have served dual and conflicting purposes. On the one hand, our public schools pay homage to a vision based on core concepts of public control, high standards, and equal access so that all children can develop their potential and become contributing, productive members of our democratic society. At the same time, our schools are infamous for replicating and exacerbating this country's undeniable stratifications based on class and race.

It is also essential to recognize that school reform cannot be isolated from resolving society's larger injustices. If our schools are to fulfill their promise, we must ensure that all children have the healthcare, housing, and family financial stability they need to do their best. This is not an excuse for the shortcomings of our public schools. Indeed, demanding such reforms as an essential component of good schools can reinvigorate the broader social movement.

At the same time, we must ensure that our public schools become doorways to opportunity, not barricades based on privilege. The original charter school proponents saw charters as a way to improve public education as a whole, not to split off into a separate movement or isolated niche schools. They were motivated by equity, not selectivity.

The question facing the charter school movement is whether it will fulfill its founding promise of a reform that empowers the powerless, or whether it will become a vehicle to further enrich the powerful and stratify our schools.

Creating successful schools, whether charter or traditional, is not easy. It is difficult, demanding work that requires vision, support, and resources. What is more, schools have crucial obligations not only to individual students and families, but to our society as a whole as we strive to create a multiracial democracy capable of addressing the many social, economic, and environmental issues that cloud our future.

As Rethinking Schools has often noted, public education, for all its flaws, exists because generations of people have fought to improve the future for themselves, their children, and the broader society. Whether public education continues to exist, and whether it rises to the challenges before it, remains an open question. Charters, for better or worse, will be part of the answer.

Leigh Dingerson
Barbara Miner
Bob Peterson
Stephanie Walters
March 2008

KEEPING THE PROMISE?

Charter Schools and the Values of Public Education

TED SIZER AND GEORGE WOOD

Charter schools—meant to be small, self-governing yet public institutions—were initially put forward as one of many ways to improve our public schools. Led by educators frustrated by large, bureaucratic systems seemingly immune to change, the concept was driven by a desire to innovate on behalf of children while furthering the most fundamental values of our public education system. This was especially true of efforts to create charter schools in under-resourced communities.

The belief was that creative educators, freed from myriad rules and regulations, would try new things that, if successful, would influence the entire system. An old governance structure (arguably the first "charter" was granted in 1778[1]) was grasped as a tool for progressive reform.

As with any tool, charters can be, and have been, put to many uses. Several of this book's essays look at how some charter schools have fallen short of the standards we believe should guide our system of public schools. Most disquieting are charters managed by the for-profit sector or by those more interested in abandoning public schooling. When held against the values that frame this country's commitment to public education, these charter schools fail to provide for the equitable access, public accountability, or public purpose that are claimed to be the hallmarks of our public schools. Of course, the same can be said of numerous traditional public schools, many of which are profoundly segregated by race and class, and which is why we have both committed our careers to school redesign and improvement. The point is to hold all public schools to the same standard, charter or traditional.

Charter schools also have a special obligation: to lead in demonstrating innovations in instruction, organization, curriculum, and design when it comes to improving our schools. Granted leeway from regulations, these charters are given the opportunity to experiment thoughtfully with multiple approaches to teaching and learning in ways that reflect the philosophy and guiding principles of the

3

school community. While some charters live up to this expectation, many do not.

We believe that charter schools have the potential to help lead the way in modeling the impact our public schools should have on the lives of children. Alongside more traditionally managed schools, charters can both live up to the values of our public system of education and also demonstrate innovation from which all can learn. When they have not lived up to that promise, it has often been in cases where charters have been used by those whose agenda is not to improve the public schools but to abandon them.

In this essay, we set out a framework for the debate about charters and their role in U.S. public education. We begin with briefly surveying the types of charter schools. Understanding their many shapes, often due to the political and policy climate in the various states, gives context to the failures and successes that subsequent essays in this collection will point out.[2]

We follow by proposing that four fundamental values underlie our system of public education and should guide our reform efforts, whether in traditional public or charter schools. Finally, we pose five questions that can provide a lens to view the profiles that make up this volume, whether of Ohio, Washington, D.C., New Orleans, Boston, or the community-based charters highlighted in the sixth chapter. Our hope is that we can come to common ground on how to assess the future of charter schools, a future based not upon the entrepreneurial aspirations of a few, but upon our shared commitment to public education.

Charters in All Shapes and Sizes

Charter schools come in many sizes, shapes, and forms, thus making it difficult to generalize about their work and their place within our system of public education. There are "stand alone" charters—publicly approved and run schools that reflect the teaching and learning values of a particular community. Examples include not only the charter schools highlighted in this book but also the Francis W. Parker Charter Essential School, in Devens, Mass.; The New City Charter School in Long Beach, Calif.; Amy Biehl Charter School in Albuquerque, N.M.; and Young Women's Leadership School in Chicago.

Next are "franchise" charters—national networks of schools based on a particular model and supported by nonprofit organizations. The Knowledge Is Power Program (KIPP) is such a "franchise" operation and currently runs dozens of schools across the country based on a common program of academics and school structure and overseen by locally constituted boards. KIPP works with local communities to raise funds for each school's startup, does national fundraising to support their programs, and provides for leadership and teacher training.

Third are "private" charters—schools run by for-profit firms. Edison Schools and White Hat Management are such "private" operators, basically taking over and running schools or providing alternative educational placements for students. As private corporations they do not have local boards and often are not required to report publicly on how they spend public funds. These schools are often controlled by individuals whose agenda is to move public education into the private marketplace.

There are hybrids of all three that seem to defy easy categorization, such as schools that are grouped together by sharing a charter management organization that takes care of backroom (payroll, benefits, etc.) operations. These management organizations may have a particular approach to education (such as the Green Dot schools in Los Angeles, with a progressive approach) or they may be solely about helping any and all charters, whatever their educational philosophies.

Finally there is a large and varied group of schools that operate as schools of choice within a school system but which have not been granted charter status. These small and largely self-governing schools—such as the "Pilot Schools" in Boston—usually operate in larger cities including New York, Chicago, and Oakland, Calif. Given varying amounts of autonomy from district rules and regulations, these schools usually have local boards and attempt to model school practices from which other district schools may learn.

Regardless of individual school differences in style or substance, the public must ask whether the charter school movement as a whole (or perhaps movements) is living up to its promise. Has it been used as a tool to strengthen and improve our system of public education, or as a device to erode this most cherished of institutions? The answer depends upon how well each form of charters or public choices adheres to the widely accepted democratic values embodied in our nation's commitment to a free and equal education for all.

Fundamental Values

Four fundamental values underlie our system of public education: *equity, access, public purpose,* and *public ownership*. Each makes substantial demands on communities and educators, requirements all too often overlooked when we talk about school outcomes or results.

Equity, a value enshrined in our nation's founding documents, requires this country to provide children with a public, "equal opportunity" education. This commitment has been reiterated through legal and legislative battles as it regards women, people of color, and those with special educational needs, and helps define our national political and social character. The equity struggle has a thorny history, as the United States continues to struggle with the notion that equity may not mean "equal," but rather that each child should have access to the educational resources he or she needs to be successful.

Access is equity's twin. It is hard to imagine an equitable system of education that does not give all participants access to the best the educational system has to offer.

Good schools should not be seen as a scarce resource to which only some families or communities have access; rather, they should be a plentiful commodity open to all children regardless of any personal or socioeconomic characteristic.

Public schools are to serve a *public purpose* as well: to prepare people to be self-governing. The top-down model of many school districts serves as a poor example of this value. Our schools are to be the place where all citizens gain the skills for lifelong learning and engaged citizenship, giving them the tools to choose wisely among leaders and programs.

Finally, schools—one of our most democratic of institutions—are to be *owned* by the public and run by local boards of laypeople who provide not only funding but facilities and support for children and their teachers. This country's long-standing vision was that public schools were to be governed closest to the people they served, requiring little need to trek to the state or federal capital for redress of grievances.

The failure of so many systems of public education to live up to these principles helped give rise to the charter movement. Too many systems were clearly unequal, with children in our poorest neighborhoods facing eroding resources for education as "white flight" drew property wealth out of central cities. In many urban areas, schools in low-income neighborhoods were the least engaging, with the poorest facilities and the least prepared teachers. Many progressive educators also found that the public purpose of these neglected schools was being given short shrift, as districts focused increasingly on test scores and discipline as criteria of school success and neglected programs and policies that engaged students to become active citizens. Finally, many educators and parents found that they no longer, if ever, "owned" their schools. In the name of efficiency and easily supervised standardization, the number of school districts shrunk and their boards, not surprisingly, became "strangers" to the community.

Many educators and parents, faced with large, impersonal bureaucracies more interested in following rules than responding to community needs, looked for a way out of the centralized muddle. Concurrently, a growing number of educators were chafing at the limits of school bureaucracies and their reluctance to embrace change. Motivated by the work of the Coalition of Essential Schools, James Comer's School Development Program, the League of Democratic Schools, and others, they wanted to engage in practices that did not necessarily fit district and state rules. While wanting to escape "the system," they nevertheless wanted to remain public schools. Public charters seemed to offer the best solution.

Enhancing Public School Values

In this context, charter schools sought to enhance the fundamental values that underlie our public school system, not to buck them. They would strive to be equitable, even in the face of systemwide inequities. They would work to use staff and resources in innovative ways to provide each child with a personalized education. They would increase options for parents to access outstanding schools, often located in the poorest communities and neighborhoods. They would stand close to the public mission of schools, centering lifelong learning and engaged citizenship in their mission. And they would be truly publicly owned, with a local system of governance that actively engaged all members of the community and that was open to public monitoring and accountability.

Much of this intent is seen in the work of Minnesota's Joe Nathan, who many credit with launching the first modern-day charter options. Nathan included the following principles, among others, in his criteria for charters:

- Charters are public, nonsectarian, free, and open to all without any admissions tests or criteria.
- The charter school will follow all civil rights laws and analogous democratic restraint.
- The charter frees up the school from rules about curriculum, management, and teaching in return for transparent accountability for results.

- The school is a school of choice; no one, student or teacher, is forced to attend.
- The school is a discrete entity, with its own board and site management.
- Employees have the right to organize and bargain collectively.
- The full per-pupil allocation of funds follows students to the charter.
- Teachers who join the charter are given the flexibility to return to the regular system and participate in programs such as state teacher retirement systems.

Within such a framework, charters would embody a core concept of a democracy—the right to petition the government for a redress of grievances. Citizens and educators who imagined a better way to educate their children could request a "charter" to run a school.

Five Guiding Questions

As noted in the beginning of this essay, it is not possible to consider charters as a single entity. What we can do is to set forward a series of questions linked to the enduring values of our public system of schooling (equity, access, public purpose, and public ownership). We also raise one additional question about the promise of charter schools to use freedom from regulation to innovate and show how public schooling can work for all citizens. Asking anything less would be to simply admit that charters are an "escape" with no other intent but to drain from the public system the most able teachers, parents, and students.

We approach this task from different backgrounds. Ted Sizer has had the experience of helping launch or actually leading two charter schools; George Wood works in a traditional public school. But we both share a commitment to the principles we have outlined above. Equally important, we do not believe our questions should be limited to charters, but must be asked of every school and every system of public education. We are not advocating a "higher" standard for charters—or their traditional cousins—when it comes to core values. We fear that for both traditional and charter schools, the democratic agenda of equity, access, public purpose, and public ownership has eroded in recent decades.

The questions that follow frame a policy discussion that could allow communities to use charters, should they choose to do so, in the interests of expanding our commitment to democracy and education. By examining how providers of charter schools have reacted to varying policy environments, we can inform the reconsideration of charter legislation and regulation in ways that increase the possibility that charter schools will live up to their promise, an issue Linda Darling-Hammond takes up in the concluding chapter of this book.

Question One: *Are charter schools strategically used within a district to provide for more equitable treatment of students?*

Equity, as we have pointed out above, does not mean "the same." Young people come to school with varying needs and abilities, and the promise of equity is about meeting each student where she or he is and moving that student to a shared standard. This may require unequal distribution of resources, but it is an inequality carried out in the name of equity.

Equity begins with the admission of students to the schoolhouse itself. One of the great hallmarks of our public education system is that the doors to the school are open to every student. No child is turned away due to race, gender, socioeconomic status, special education needs, or prior record. Most unfortunately, as a nation our commitment to equity and access in public education has diminished—whether through housing patterns that segregate families by socioeconomic and racial characteristics or Supreme Court decisions which undermine equal access to educational resources. While charters alone cannot overturn this pattern, they should not exacerbate it. Thus, when charters are added to any system of public education, their doors must be open to all students.

Among the ways in which schools limit equal access and violate the principle of equity is through admissions tests or other measures to screen children. (We acknowledge that too often public school systems fail this test through devices such as "exam schools" or "magnet schools" with various screening criteria.) Children and their families may certainly choose schools based on interests, pedagogic styles, or grade configurations. But children should never be turned away from their public school of choice. Doing so violates a public system of education, and if charters are allowed to use such screening mechanisms, this immediately calls into question the purpose of the charters granted.

Schools also screen students by making demands upon a child's family in order to be admitted. Insisting that families sign a "commitment form" or "contract" to commit time or financial resources to the school only exacerbates the current inequities in our system of public education. While parent involvement is important in any child's education, such a requirement ensures that some schools serve only those children from the most intact and financially favored families.

Equity also extends into the fabric of the daily life in the school, and demands that all students have full access, within reason, to all programs. Students with special needs must be accommodated and students with particular talents should be encouraged to go beyond the normal standards. Any charter or system of charters that does not provide for accommodation for students' learning challenges is no longer working within the spirit and intent of public education. Charters, along with all public schools, should ensure that they are not turning away students who are English language learners, struggle with behavioral issues, or who bring with them the wide range of challenging issues our children often face.

Question Two: *Do charter schools provide for greater access to strong schools and a range of educational opportunities for all families in the community?*

Any system of schooling should operate so that state and local resources are equitably distributed. It is not fair to require some public schools to operate on budgets that are vastly less than the budgets of others. This is one of the more volatile issues in public education, given this country's willingness to allow extremes of wealth and poverty to create separate systems vastly inequitable in the resources provided for children—"rich" public schools sitting just across boundary lines from vastly underresourced schools. In fact, the evidence is abundantly clear that our poorest children receive the fewest educational resources despite their greater need. While charter schools are not a device for overcoming this conundrum perplexing our society at large, they should lead to ever more equitable schools serving all families.

If charter schools are to be part of the mix of schools in a community, access to those charters must be guaranteed for all the community's families and children. The United States seems to have acquiesced to the notion that good schools are to be treated as a scarce resource, and those with the highest income levels or the ability to seek out the best choices are provided the best schools. Lacking either the resources or personal capital to find such schools, everyone else is shuffled off to what is left. This has led to a concentration of our most needy students and challenged families in schools that are underresourced and lack a drawing card.

Issues of access, as with those of equity, bedevil our entire system and charters will not, in and of themselves, alter this. At the least, however, they should not make the problem worse. For example, given the distortions embedded in most contemporary sorting systems, if charters use admission criteria such as test scores or prior behavior records, they will automatically narrow access to the most able and wealthy. Additionally, the location of charters may dictate who can attend. Finally, the ability of families to make wise choices about the school their children attend clearly varies by the amount of stress under which the families operate.

If issues of access are not addressed in a public system utilizing charters, there is no doubt that there will be a "creaming" of the most supported students. Families who have the wherewithal to attend recruiting meetings, read materials provided by school districts, visit multiple schools around the city, or talk to parents who have made similar choices, will be better situated to take advantage of charters or choices. The research on student success and familial involvement is so extensive it is not worth recounting here. The point is, unless all families have the support to access multiple choices in a system, charters become one more way in which we sort the haves from the have-nots in our schools.

It seems logical to us that any public school system that uses charter schools would have to involve structural changes in order to guarantee access. First, the system must provide a wide enough range of good choices so that no child is "dumped" into a school of last resort. In other words, every school should be a choice and a good one at that. Second, institutional barriers to attending/choosing good schools should be removed, including any screening devices. Third, families must be provided with the supports that make choosing a school a reality. This would involve teachers within the system providing families with information about their choices, including through parent education and neighborhood outreach programs.

As with any attempt to design a system consistent with our democratic principles, charter schools must be granted the wise exceptions we cherish in our society. In terms of equity and access, this means there may be carefully watched and monitored exceptions such as schools that serve only girls or only boys. These sometimes controversial exceptions are granted only to fulfill the innovative role that charters portend to play, and are discussed in more detail below.

Question Three: *Does the use of charter schools further the purpose of public education, to provide all our children with the tools necessary for lifelong learning and engaged citizenship?*

A public education is just that, education in the name of the public. Anything less is merely training. Thus, public schools must first operate within the framework of providing the broad liberal arts agenda that serves the public interest. This means children will be developing those skills that are traditionally associated with civic intelligence, the ability to exercise judgment about the issues we face as a nation and society. Unfortunately, we have not, as a nation, had a careful discussion of what skills, knowledge, and abilities make for lifelong learners and engaged citizens. Rather, we have relied upon a system of standardized measures of content knowledge to dominate what we believe our children should learn. If charters (or Pilot Schools or any other innovative model for that matter) are to do the work of innovation that has been claimed for them, they need to be genuinely freed from bureaucratic restrictions. One of the possibilities would be to grant, in their charters, freedoms to find new ways to assess student development as opposed to relying on existing standardized tests. Perhaps nothing is more stifling to sound educational practices than the narrow focus on standardized test scores. Freed from this limitation, could charters provide the leadership on new ways to assess students and hold schools accountable for something more than the ability to fill in a bubble sheet?

Our point is that all schools must either play by the same rules or be involved in rewriting the rules in ways that hold us to even higher notions of educational accountability. We believe that the latter is possible, and that charters could take the lead on this.

Question Four: *Do the charter schools operate as publicly owned schools, with full transparency and community governance?*

Democracy is not only what we teach; it is also what we do. Public schools are creations of communities and spend public dollars. They must be both responsive to local input through formal and informal measures and completely transparent in how they spend public dollars. So must it be for charters.

Genuine public ownership requires the ability to locally oversee the school and for students, educators, and parents to have input into programmatic and policy changes. In fact, many charter schools feel that they are responsive to such input, as parents may leave if their concerns are not addressed. And yet this raises a very delicate paradox. If charters are to take on a distinctive character, how are they to hold on to that character if the participants within the school begin to push for changes that would alter the nature of the school? On one hand, the charter is a choice, and by its nature may not be the choice for all families. On the other, if it is a public school it cannot choose which public it wants to serve.

Additionally, how does the charter school address parent and/or student grievances? In traditional school systems there usually exists a system, albeit flawed at times, for members of the school community to appeal school rulings or practices. But the potential exists in a charter that such complainants could merely be asked to leave the school, a not-too-subtle way to squash dissent.

There is no easy resolution of this problem. The potential danger is that charters will have the ability to "push out" students or families they do not like, similar to what happens in private schools and specialized public schools. On the other hand, charters cannot engage in too much of this behavior or they will lose their student base.

An additional issue around public ownership is one of transparency in the school's operation. A public school is a public trust, and that trust must be validated by openness (except, of course, where students' rights to privacy must be protected). Information on finances, curriculum, assessment, teacher qualifications, program, student demographics, and other operational issues must be widely and publicly available. This information about any school that receives public funds must not only be shared with the school community, but also with the public at large, and must always be subject to commentary.

Question Five: *The reason charters are granted exemptions to rules is to demonstrate a better way to educate children from which all parts of the system can learn. Thus we must ask, do the public policies that authorize charters provide genuine regulatory relief, as well as a system to report widely on their innovations and results?*

There needs to be genuine regulatory relief for charters and any other school that wants to take on the challenge of innovation. As Ted Sizer has written, "(A)ny policy that drives charters into old molds—making them, in effect, 'look and act familiar' as worthy expressions of the existing 'system,' producing students who do well primarily on tests organized in ways that reflect this system—undermines the sound intent of the charter idea."[3] It is not enough to offer charters the ability to design curriculum, schedules, and staffing patterns; they must also be allowed to innovate with assessment and accountability systems. And yet according to the Education Commission of the States, all of the charter laws in this nation require that the state's standards and assessments be applied to charter schools.[4]

Nothing drives schools as much as state assessments linked to the federal reauthorization in 2002 of the Elementary and Secondary

Education Act (titled No Child Left Behind). Without the freedom to innovate when it comes to such mandates, the ability of any school to inform change in the larger system is severely limited. Given that there is so much doubt around current assessments both to drive meaningful change and reveal much about what our children are learning, it seems a fortuitous moment to offer relief from limits that seem to have little to do with educating and much to do with standardizing. Perhaps charters (and their partners) could answer the age-old question of how to have standards without standardization. Further, it would seem that charter advocates could help foster more innovation by joining the national movement to challenge the testing and sanctions agenda of the so-called standards movement. This would be a major contribution.

In addition, any charter authorization should mandate that innovation and dissemination of innovative practices be part and parcel of the work of the charter. This was the intent of charters and yet in many charter systems, particularly those premised on "competition" rather than collaboration, it has been forgotten. Currently the only rule about innovation seems to be that the charter can do what it wants if it meets the same regulatory standards that other schools must meet in terms of test scores. Certainly this encourages the unscrupulous behavior of some charter operators to "cream off" particular students who are more likely to do well on standardized measures.

Simply doing more of the same is not an option. Rather, a new, promising approach must be part of the research and development agenda of the school. Such approaches could be structural, such as preserving a small school or a nongraded elementary program; curricular, in being based in community service or integrated across fields; or evaluative, in relying upon performance assessment. Regardless, they must offer a new way of seeing the work of the schools and be transferable to any and all schools. The system must also support the evaluation and dissemination of such practices, whether they come from the public or charter sector. The work of the Sizer Teacher Center at the Francis W. Parker Charter School, with its national outreach efforts to educators and parents, is a strong example of this type of practice.

Furthermore, since many charter schools work to provide models for the public system, charters must reflect the realities of the public system in terms of the demographics of their students and families, the resources they bring to their work with students, and their willingness to engage in public dialogue and disclosure about their work. Only when charters truly reflect the population at large will they have lessons to share with the rest of the educational system.

Our sense is that the fundamental reason for charters, to demonstrate innovation and promising practices from which all public schools might learn, has been lost by many of the policy makers and officials in whom we have placed our trust to develop the concept of charter schooling. Rather than a way to inform change within the larger system, in many cases charter schools have been rushed into operation, allowed to expand without careful evaluation, and presented as an escape from the public district schools. It is no surprise then that charters are becoming a political football that have not shown, in spite of notable exceptions, any overall ability to better educate children.[5] We feel that the loss of the innovative drive behind charters is the greatest lost promise of all. It need not be this way. With thoughtful changes, public school systems can use charter schools as the innovative engine they were designed to be.

Among the profiles that follow, that of New Orleans demonstrates perhaps the overriding lesson of the charter school experience to date: How charter schools emerge and function in any given city, district, or state is a feature of the political maneuvering that takes place around the authorizing and implementation process. Whether these processes are guided by a commitment to equity, access, public purpose, and public ownership will make all the difference in terms of how well our public schools serve our children. What seems clear to us from these profiles is that charter schools may be a part of the mix in improving our public schools, but if, and only if, they are part of a genuinely public system of education.

TED SIZER IS THE FOUNDER OF THE COALITION OF ESSENTIAL SCHOOLS (CES) AND THE AUTHOR OF THE THREE HORACE BOOKS THAT DESCRIBE THE EARLY YEARS OF CES. HE IS PROFESSOR EMERITUS AT BROWN UNIVERSITY, WHERE HE WAS CHAIR OF THE EDUCATION DEPARTMENT FROM 1984-1989, AND IS CURRENTLY A VISITING PROFESSOR AT HARVARD AND BRANDEIS UNIVERSITIES. HE AND HIS WIFE NANCY RECENTLY SERVED AS THE ACTING CO-PRINCIPALS OF THE FRANCIS W. PARKER CHARTER ESSENTIAL SCHOOL IN DEVENS, MASS. HIS LATEST BOOK, *WHAT IS SCHOOL: CONVICTIONS FROM EXPERIENCE*, WILL BE PUBLISHED IN 2008.

GEORGE WOOD IS DIRECTOR OF THE FORUM FOR EDUCATION AND DEMOCRACY AND PRINCIPAL OF FEDERAL HOCKING HIGH SCHOOL IN STEWART, OHIO. HE WAS RECENTLY THE CHAIR OF THE EDUCATION TRANSITION TEAM FOR THEN

GOVERNOR-ELECT TED STRICKLAND OF OHIO. HE IS THE AUTHOR OF *SCHOOLS THAT WORK*, *A TIME TO LEARN* AND EDITOR OF *MANY CHILDREN LEFT BEHIND*. IN ADDITION, HE HAS AUTHORED OVER 100 ARTICLES AND ANNUALLY SPEAKS TO DOZENS OF EDUCATIONAL GATHERINGS.

Endnotes

1. Sizer, T. (ed.), *The Age of the Academies* (New York: Teachers College, 1964).
2. Since the provision of public schooling is left to each state, charter schools are authorized under state legislation. At this time, 40 states and the District of Columbia have legislation that allows for the creation of charter schools.
3. Sizer, T., "Don't Tie Us Down: Charters Are for Choice and Must Be Given the Freedom to Experiment," *Education Next*, 2005, vol. 3.
4. Education Commission of the States, *State Notes: Charter Schools*, April 2003.
5. "Charter School Scores," *American School Board Journal 2007 Educational Vital Signs*, March 2007, p. 7.

Unlovely:
How the Market Is Failing
The Children of New Orleans

LEIGH DINGERSON

> "What the best and wisest parent wants for his own child, that must the community want for all of its children. Any other ideal for our schools is narrow and unlovely; acted upon, it destroys our democracy."
> —John Dewey, *The School and Society*, 1907

> A child playing on a flood-ravaged New Orleans street six months after Katrina was asked by a reporter why he wasn't in school. "I don't go to school," he replied. "My mama tried to put us in school and nobody would take us, so we don't go to school."[1]
> —Salon.com, Feb. 13, 2006

When Hurricane Katrina slammed into the Gulf coast in August 2005, the storm shattered the New Orleans public school system. Over half of the district's buildings were destroyed and the students and staff were dispersed across the nation.

But the storm was only the beginning of a more fundamental transition. In the weeks following Katrina, with the city's residents stunned and displaced, the foundation was laid for a new type of school system—a market-based system where schools compete against each other, families and students are cast as consumers, and those who don't make it in the "market" are allowed to fall through the cracks.

The implications of this experiment emerged even before the first anniversary of the storm that blew privatization into the New Orleans schools.

Embattled System, Overlooked Children

Before Katrina, the New Orleans Public Schools was a struggling district of 63,000 students. Over the years, most white families had retreated to neighboring parishes or to private schools. Middle-class and professional African-American families relied heavily on the city's many Catholic schools. Drained of this middle-class constituency and the political support that it provided, the New Orleans public schools were in crisis. The Orleans Parish School Board, the elected governing body for the New Orleans Public Schools, had long been dysfunctional, wracked with corruption, mismanagement, and lack of vision. Bright spots existed, and student performance was in fact improving in 2005. But the pervasive conviction persisted that the system was broken beyond repair. The Louisiana Department of Education, meanwhile, had decided that the New Orleans schools needed fundamental reorganization. No doubt they recognized the political sensitivity of wresting a public school system from local hands, but they had started. In 2003 the legislature took control of four low-performing New Orleans schools and turned them over to independent charter operators.

Katrina provided the excuse that the state Department of Education needed to move to scale. When the levees broke, the floods that inundated the city left most of the population homeless and scattered; among them, thousands of public school students, their families, and the district's 7,500 employees.

The utter ineptitude of the federal response to the hurricane sparked anger across the country. But some watched through a decidedly different lens. Paul Hill with the Center on Reinventing Public Education wrote just three weeks after the storm: "In the case of post-hurricane New Orleans, American school planners will be as close as they have ever come to a 'green field' opportunity."[2]

A Powerful Message for Desperate Communities

Many of those who saw green in New Orleans were members of the Education Industry Association, which represents corporations that sell services to schools and school districts. Others included conservative think tanks like the Thomas B. Fordham Foundation and the Heritage Foundation. For years, these institutions have argued that public schools ought to be run more like businesses (or even *by* businesses). With the emergence of charter schools in the early 1990s, these reformers saw a strategy to test their ideas. Independently operated charter schools, they asserted, could demonstrate the efficiencies of a system based on choice and competition. Conveniently, such a model would also create a multi-billion dollar market for the services some of them sell.

These charter advocates have an impressive capacity to ply their ideological wares. Well-financed and politically well-connected, their movement has strategically targeted underresourced urban school systems. In these struggling districts, with declining participation and support from the middle class, the pitch for independent schools as the escape route is a powerful tonic. The elixir of "choice" serves the privatizers' interests. It sets up an individualized escape route that not only divides communities, but also weakens the political will for collective action in support of public schools. It becomes a self-fulfilling prophecy: The more highly motivated and engaged families pull out (taking public dollars with them), the worse the public schools get. The worse they get, the more appealing the escape route. This fundamental logic is at the core of the conservative agenda to convert public education to a private, free-market system.

Less than two decades after the concept of charter schools caught hold, the political, policy, and public relations operations of the charter school movement are almost entirely controlled by its conservative wing. Their objective is the deregulated growth of independent charter schools, dependent on private services and management but supported with public dollars.

New Orleans was a feast, laid out before them on Aug. 29, 2005.

Seeing Green Fields in a Muddy City

Within days of Katrina, well-connected interests lobbied in Baton Rouge and met privately in Washington with U.S. Education Secretary Margaret Spellings.

Their message was clear: the storm presents an opportunity—a "defining moment in history," according to the president of the Education Industry Association—to create a new paradigm for public education. There was much talk of a "clean slate," as if the histories of families, students, teachers, and communities could be wiped away by a flood, never to haunt a privatized rebuilding effort.

The dismantling of the New Orleans Public Schools began before the floodwaters receded. Within two weeks of the hurricane, Secretary Spellings sent a letter to state superintendents across the country announcing that charter schools were "uniquely equipped" to serve students displaced by Katrina and that she would waive federal restrictions on charter schools in order to help New Orleans. Two weeks later, she announced the first of two charter school grants of more than $20 million each to Louisiana.

That October, Louisiana Governor Kathleen Babineaux Blanco waived key portions of the state's charter school law in order to facilitate privatization. One of the waived provisions required staff and parent approval when converting a traditional public school to a charter.[3] Her order allowed public schools to be converted without the input—or even the knowledge—of parents and teachers. It remains in effect today, over two years after the storm.

Just after Thanksgiving in 2005, the state legislature took over 107 New Orleans Public Schools, leaving only four schools under the direct control of the Orleans Parish School Board. In February 2006, the school board fired all 7,500 teachers, custodians, cafeteria workers, and other unionized employees of the district.

In a few short months, the infrastructure of the New Orleans Public Schools had been deconstructed and a new framework built. Three types of publicly funded schools made up the new landscape:

- Charter schools, operated by independent corporations, groups, or networks.
- Orleans Parish (New Orleans Public) schools, still under the direct jurisdiction of the locally elected school board.
- Recovery School District schools, operated directly by the state's Board of Elementary and Secondary Education.

This new framework promised "choice" for individual families and "competition" which—according to the theory—would force the public schools to improve. The city's historic and powerful teacher union, meanwhile, had been devastated by Katrina and barely a voice was lifted in protest.

Louisiana's Charter School Demonstration Program, passed in 1997, didn't foretell the use of charters to deconstruct public education. The purpose of charters, according to the law,[4] is to allow the creation of "innovative kinds of independent public schools" that will "improve pupil learning and, *in general, the public school system*" (author's emphasis), "increase learning opportunities and access to quality education for pupils," and "encourage the use of different and innovative teaching methods."

The possibility existed in post-Katrina New Orleans for local communities to help rebuild their schools. But there was no effort to engage residents of New Orleans. Instead, national organizations swept in to take charge of the process.

Naomi Klein, in her 2007 book *The Shock Doctrine*, describes this process as "disaster capitalism": "The original disaster—the coup, the terrorist attack, the market meltdown, the war, the tsunami, the hurricane—puts the entire population into a state of collective shock. The falling bombs, the bursts of terror, the pounding winds serve to soften up whole societies. ... [S]hocked societies often give up things they would otherwise fiercely protect."[5]

In New Orleans, there was the added fact that the majority of public school families had fled the city. By the time they began to return, the coup was largely a done deal.

Speculation and Exclusion

With federal money flowing for charter schools and no money for rebuilding the old public system, the local and state boards set about opening as many charters as possible, as quickly as possible. There was no coordinated vision or plan for how the system they were building would serve children well and equitably. No one seemed to consider how to provide access to children in all corners of the city. There were no pedagogical strategies. The only strategy seemed to be to let a thousand entrepreneurial efforts bloom.

One of the first school proposals came from pre-existing Lusher K-6 charter school in the city's affluent and well-connected Garden District. The group had unsuccessfully sought permission the previous year to expand their charter school. Just a month after Katrina, the Lusher board appealed for permission to open a second campus, extend their school through 12th grade, and prioritize enrollment for the children of faculty members at nearby Tulane University. On Oct. 7, just weeks after the flood and in the absence of any community hearings or public debate, the Orleans Parish School Board (meeting 70 miles outside New Orleans in Baton Rouge), not only permitted Lusher's expansion, but also agreed to hand over the historic Alcee Fortier High School building to accommodate their added grades.

Across the river on the west bank of the Mississippi, where the storm damage had been minimal, another early proposal was submitted by Brian Riedlinger, CEO of the School Leadership Center of Greater New Orleans, a training program for school administrators. Riedlinger proposed to run all 13 schools on the city's west bank as the Algiers Charter Schools Association and promised that eight schools would be open before the winter was over. At the same meeting where the board turned over Fortier High School to Lusher, they also blessed Riedlinger's takeover of the west bank schools.

Meanwhile, the state's Board of Elementary and Secondary Education was suddenly in control of over 100 New Orleans schools and dozens of unusable buildings. They had created the Recovery School District to operate a few New Orleans schools—now they were sitting on virtually the entire district. The Board appointed an inexperienced superintendent and assumed the duties of a local district, even though they were based in Baton Rouge and the elected board's 11 members included only two from New Orleans. Their plan was to grant charters to as many of the schools under their control as possible. Unsure how to proceed, they looked outside of New Orleans and Louisiana for guidance. The conservative wing of the charter movement was there to help.

The board turned to the Chicago-based National Association of Charter School Authorizers (NACSA) to manage the screening and evaluation of charter proposals. Allowing a group hundreds of miles away to choose which charter applications were approved in New Orleans may have been expedient, given the post-storm chaos. But it also disadvantaged community groups that wanted to reopen their local schools. Though state law requires charter applicants to be nonprofit organizations, there is no prohibition against subcontracting with external management corporations. Indeed, it soon became clear that virtually the only route to a successful application was through a highly resourced collaboration.

One exception was Dr. Martin Luther King, Jr. Charter School for Science and Technology. The school was a community institution in the now-devastated Lower 9th Ward. After the storm, the longtime principal, Doris Roché-Hicks, and dozens of parents and teachers quickly put together a proposal to reopen MLK as a charter school. Roché-Hicks didn't like the idea of charter schools, but knew it was the only way to get MLK up and running. While federal money was available—$2,000 per student—for the opening of charter schools, there was no money to reopen a traditional school.

As fall turned to winter, more charter schools were authorized, both by the Orleans Parish School Board and by the Recovery School District. Though the official applicants were usually local nonprofit organizations (many of them created for the sole purpose of applying for a charter), many of the schools were subcontracted to national management groups. The for-profit Leona Group, based in Detroit, got two schools. NACSA members SABIS International and Mosaica Education got schools. The Knowledge Is Power Program (KIPP), based in San Francisco, won contracts to operate two schools during the 2006-07 school year, and opened a third after that.

Facilities were the next big challenge. Any school buildings that were relatively unscathed by the storm were the focus of intense speculation. The state board hired out-of-state contractors to clear out buildings that had been evacuated just a week into the 2005-06 school year. Everything went, regardless of storm damage: desks, computers, whole libraries of books. Personal items and memories went too: trophies, band instruments, locker contents, paperweights, and artwork. Even in buildings untouched by the flooding, slates were wiped clean.

In February 2007, I stood outside Thurgood Marshall Middle School in Mid-City, getting a tour of empty school buildings from neighborhood resident Amy Lafont as part of research I was doing for the Center for Community Change. While we were talking, a pick-up truck with Texas plates pulled up. Three men got out and began taking pictures of the building. When asked, the men said they were deciding whether to bid on a contract to renovate the school. "The community hasn't heard anything about what's going to happen to our school," said Lafont. "Is it going to be reopened?" The contractors said they had no information. Less than five minutes later, another car pulled up, and another team of people emerged and began taking pictures. They were looking for a facility to house their newly authorized charter school, approved to open in the fall of 2007 and operated by the New York-based Edison Schools, the nation's largest for-profit education management organization.

In the nearby DeSaix neighborhood, residents waited to hear about the future of their elementary school, Langston Hughes. While they waited, a new nonprofit called NOLA 180 was advertising on the internet for staff and administrators for the new Langston Hughes Academy Charter School. The school opened in July 2007, drawing its 123 4th and 5th graders from across the city.

Observers in New Orleans noticed that many of the same faces, often developers, could be found on several charter school boards. In the case of the emerging Langston Hughes Academy, for example, the chairman of the board was also the principal at S.J. Green Charter School, and concurrently served as president of the Louisiana Charter School Association. The head of NOLA 180 is a former national staff member of KIPP, who had moved to New Orleans in 2005.

Closed Doors and Safety Nets
By the spring of 2006, only 25 public schools had opened in New Orleans. Eighteen (72 percent) were charter schools, and 10 (40 percent) had selective admissions policies. Many of the schools were quickly filled.

Getting a child into a school had become dizzyingly complicated. Registration was handled at each individual charter school building (the Algiers network provided a centralized enrollment process), so parents were forced to crisscross the city to find spaces. There had been no oversight to ensure that schools were opening in geographic proximity to the places where returning families were living, and neighborhood schools did not guarantee neighborhood students a seat. Hundreds of parents faced a daily commute to deliver children to schools across town, as most charter schools had not begun to offer transportation even though state law requires it.

Questions of access emerged as soon as the school doors swung open. Or, perhaps more appropriately, as doors swung shut. By late January 2006, the NAACP had filed suit, charging that dozens of students—mostly students with disabilities—had been turned away from charter schools. These charges continued to surface throughout the spring.[6] Most charters quickly recruited the number of students they were originally contracted to serve, and then closed their doors. Stories spread of schools discouraging registration by students they deemed high risk, either because of disabilities, behavioral problems, or other concerns.

As more families returned to the still largely nonfunctioning city, there was an indisputable shortage of seats. Frustration grew. A full year after the storm, one exasperated mother at the Recovery School District headquarters asked a reporter, "Why am I still sitting here begging to get a child into school?"[7]

Many looked to the state-run Recovery School District to provide access to all returning students. The Recovery district had opened three schools in early 2006, and was hoping to charter out the bulk of the additional schools under its control. But the authorizing process went more slowly than anticipated.

When the 2005-06 school year sputtered to a close in June, all eyes turned to August, hopeful that the first full school year since Katrina would be smoother. Later that month, the state board overseeing the Recovery district issued a list of 53 New Orleans schools that would open for 2006-07. Of these:

- Five were operated directly by the Orleans Parish School Board (four of those as selective admissions schools).
- Seventeen were operated directly by the state, as the Recovery School District.
- Eight were part of the Algiers Charter School network.
- The remaining 23 were charters authorized either by the state or Orleans Parish.

An astounding 58 percent of the "public" schools were charters. In one short year, New Orleans had become home to the highest concentration of charter schools in the nation.

Despite the growing number of schools, access remained a huge problem. While not officially considered selective, some of the new charter schools engage in practices that raise concerns about "creaming." The two KIPP schools, for example, use the national "KIPP Commitment to Excellence Form."[8] All prospective parents and students must sign, accepting KIPP's program of extended days, Saturday school twice a month, and summer sessions. It also commits parents to reading to their child nightly, and being available to the school at all times. Finally, the contract includes a strict code for student behavior and warns that failure to adhere to the commitments by either the parents or student may result in the child's dismissal.

In a 2006 study, researchers in Maryland[9] expressed concern that such contracts might "undermine the spirit of open enrollment policies." They also found that some schools asked students to leave, not just if the children stepped off the path, but also if parents failed to comply with the contract.

Another powerful factor in New Orleans has been the operating agreements between charter schools and their authorizer, which allow the schools to limit enrollment. Unlike traditional public schools, which must guarantee students a seat in their neighborhood school, New Orleans charter schools have been permitted to cap their enrollment and maintain a student-to-teacher ratio of 20:1. Students returning to New Orleans in the late summer and early fall of 2006 often found themselves shut out of the most promising schools. Over half the operating schools were charters, and they were filled to capacity. Hundreds of students were returning weekly, but the only "choice" available was one of the 42 percent of school buildings that remained open to all. Particularly hard hit was the city's large population of children with special needs or disabilities. These students saw school doors closed to them. Still, proponents proclaimed success. "New Orleans is such a great example of what you can do if you start over," chirped Jeanne Allen, founder of the pro-charter Center for Education Reform.[10]

The new market-driven structure exacerbated disparities between the "haves" and the "have-nots"—between the children with savvy parents and those who slipped through the cracks or were turned away from charter schools. Unlike in the business world, however, public education has to have a way to serve "customers" shut out of the market.

In August 2006, there wasn't any such safety net. The state-run Recovery School District had not assumed that it would operate more

than a handful of schools itself. When it became clear that an insufficient number of charter seats would be available to accommodate
returning students, the Recovery district needed to step up to the
plate. Incredibly, it had no plan for doing so.

In July, eight months after her appointment as head of the
Recovery School District and only one month before the start of the
2006-07 school year, Robin Jarvis acknowledged that she had yet to
hire a single teacher for the 17 Recovery District schools, and post-
poned their opening.[11] The district's chief of staff revealed[12] that
they had only 10 people on the Recovery District staff, only one of
whom was responsible for coordinating the special education program. According to the NAACP, as many as 200 special education
students had failed to find seats in the city's charter schools and
were awaiting placement in Recovery district schools.

When the schools finally opened in mid-September of 2006, six
weeks after the first charter schools opened, it was all-out chaos. Textbooks had not arrived; buildings were not furnished with desks, let
alone computers. Transportation was dysfunctional, if available.
Meals were frozen. There were far fewer teachers than classes to
teach. And some schools had the undeniable feel of prisons—where
discipline replaced academics on the agenda and security guards literally outnumbered teachers. During the early days at John McDonogh
High School ("John Mac"), students were herded into the school
gymnasium where they sat all day, guarded but not taught.

These problems continued throughout the school year. In January 2007, when newspapers reported that over 300 children had
been unable to enroll in any school, the story made the national
news. The city's charter schools however, were under no obligation
to jeopardize their 20:1 student teacher ratio and remained closed to
new students. The Recovery district rushed two additional schools
into operation, and lifted class sizes in some buildings to nearly
40:1.[13] An English teacher at John Mac reported a 7th-period English class with 53 students.

Unequal Resources: Riches and Rags

The lack of resources at the Recovery schools put a spotlight on an
inevitable feature of school districts that have been fragmented into
competing entities.

Charter schools, particularly those with ties to the national charter movement, are able to leverage external funding to enhance their
programs. Many of the charter schools in New Orleans have taken

advantage of the movement's cozy access to deep pocket philanthropies and savvy, well-connected parents to secure private funding well above the public dollars they receive. This largesse allows individual schools—and there are a lot of them in New Orleans—to spend far more per pupil than traditional public schools.

One example is Lusher Charter School. When the Lusher parents were gifted the Alcee Fortier High School for their expansion campus in October 2006, Fortier, like many other New Orleans public school buildings, was in disrepair. But Katrina put wind in some sails. As a charter facility, Fortier accessed $14 million in state dollars and supplemented with $1.5 million from Tulane University to complete a top-to-bottom renovation of the building. As former Fortier students began to trickle back into the community over the summer of 2006, they were stunned to see the feverish work underway at their school. But the elation was short lived, as they learned that the school was no longer open to them. Lusher Charter School admits students only on the basis of academic record, with first priority going to children of Tulane faculty. Former Fortier students were not welcome.

Across the river is the network of schools now operated by the Algiers Charter School Association. The initiative is heavily underwritten by the local Baptist Community Ministries—the state's largest private foundation, created by the conversion of Baptist Community Hospital from a nonprofit to a for-profit. The foundation's millions were invested in Brian Riedlinger's leadership training institute. But when Riedlinger moved to establish the Algiers Charter district, Baptist Community Ministries continued to pay his salary as Chief Educational Officer. On the strength of private support like this, the Algiers Charter School Association reported in July 2006 that it had a $12 million *reserve* fund.[14]

A few months later, the superintendent of the Recovery School District was assuring the media that her teachers were learning how to teach "creatively" given the lack of textbooks in the schools.

The disparities in resources in New Orleans wipes away any pretense that the new school system is serving children equitably. But the resource gap is troubling for another reason. An original justification for charters was to provide an opportunity for innovation using the same resources available to traditional public schools. Only then would successful practices tested in charters be realistically available to strengthen the public system that they serve. Clearly, in New Orleans, competition precluded collaboration or replication.

Winners and Losers

The presence of a significant number of charter schools draws resources of many kinds away from the traditional district. In New Orleans, the situation was exacerbated by the sudden and total destruction of virtually the entire system. But the dog-eat-dog atmosphere that emerged in the city following the storm has not served the children of New Orleans. Millions of public dollars are now being diverted out of state, to the corporate contractors hired to manage charter schools. Meanwhile, on the ground, a school system is being created in which the students' educations are separated by thousands—even millions—of dollars spent, or not spent, on them.

Allowing huge disparities in resources, sorting and separating young people, closing schoolhouse doors—all these practices send an unmistakable message to the children left behind.

Charter school proponents point out that their enrollment demographics—by race, by economic disadvantage—largely mirror those of their co-existing traditional public systems. But sorting kids is much more subtle than what can measured by income or skin color. Many in New Orleans now refer to the Recovery School District schools as "the dumping ground." Can public education meet the values set forth for it when some schools are considered "dumping grounds?" And how can those schools, over time deprived of social as well as financial resources, ever hope to compete with their better-funded charter cousins?

The teaching profession has been impacted as well. Few now dispute that high quality teaching is the most significant predictor of student achievement. What happens when market forces, rather than a commitment to the common good, determine the distribution of teachers?

The New Orleans charter schools are free to hire teachers through individual annual contracts. There is no salary schedule and no collective bargaining. Many of the charter schools opted to forgo experienced teachers in favor of young and enthusiastic college graduates with no classroom experience. But their tenure is often brief, particularly when they don't have seasoned mentors and role models to support them through their first years. Other charters, in the spirit of the marketplace, quickly recruited highly experienced and qualified teachers and offered to pay them handsomely.

Teacher recruitment for the New Orleans charter schools is supported through a website called TeachNOLA.org. A recruitment ad, posted on CareerBuilders.com by TeachNOLA in early 2007, encouraged teachers to come to New Orleans to join in the city's rebuilding. "Certified teachers will be placed in the city's charter schools. Uncertified teachers will teach in the Recovery district schools,"[15] read the ad.

At the same time, the organization's homepage sent interested applicants to two distinct sections of the website, depending on whether the candidate was fully licensed to teach or seeking certification. Uncertified teachers were offered coded, but unmistakably grim descriptions of the Recovery School District:

- "Students from any neighborhood in the city."
- The Recovery district will "absorb the swelling student population."
- Teachers must be "particularly prepared for challenges."
- "The district is committed to *accommodating* (author's emphasis) these returnees."

Fully certified teachers, on the other hand, were recruited with a much different tone:

- A "premier laboratory!"
- "An unprecedented opportunity!"
- "We expect you to be an educational pioneer whose students excel."

This is the competitive model in action, but it's unlovely for sure. Public education is premised on a commitment to excellence in all schools, not a commitment for some students to "excel" and others to be "accommodated."

Teaching in New Orleans is no longer a collective commitment. In fact, being "collective" can get you fired. In the Algiers charter schools employee handbook, for instance, disclosing the details of your compensation package is among the behaviors that may lead to termination.[16]

The original idea of charter schools was that they would innovate, try things out, and then share their successes and failures with their sponsoring public system, so as to improve public education in general. The Louisiana charter school law recognized these purposes. But competition is a different ball game. In a system based on competition, there's no premium on sharing successful models. There's no percentage in transparency. There's no profit in encouraging other schools to pick up your most successful strategies. There's not even any profit in letting other schools know what those strategies are.

The Flea Market Approach

In New Orleans, as in Ohio and the District of Columbia, the voices guiding charter schooling are not the voices of communities or educators, but of entrepreneurs who see an ideological green field—a financial pasture to plow. As James M. Huger, chairman of Lafayette Academy charter school, so precisely put it in an article in the *Atlantic Monthly* in January 2007,[17] "I'm a real-estate developer; I don't know the first thing about running a school." Huger promised prospective parents "a great product" and hired New York's for-profit Mosaica Education Inc. to deliver it.

People on both sides of the charter debate say that in concept, chartering is a governance model—a structure for the adults, not the children. But what is happening in New Orleans is not so benign. Under the tutelage of national conservative activists, the Louisiana Board of Elementary and Secondary Education opened a flea market of entrepreneurial opportunism that is dismantling the institution of public education in New Orleans. There has been no deliberation on the charter models that might be tried, or how the lessons will be shared. There is certainly no process for replicating what works in order to advance the system as a whole.

No one is defending the troubled pre-Katrina New Orleans Public Schools, and no one wants that system back. But if there had not been the rush to the charter flea market—promoted by national advocates, bankrolled by the federal government, and enabled by the state legislature and department of education—the teachers, parents, and students of New Orleans might have had the chance to reclaim and hand-hew a public school system that worked for all of them. It isn't the foundation of public education that was failing in New Orleans—there are many public schools there, and across the country, that are flourishing. We know what it takes. What was lacking was the commitment to make it happen for impoverished, African-American students. And it's still lacking.

What emerged after Katrina is inherently inequitable. The "new" model requires a safety net to catch the children who are pushed out of, or never make it through, the game of so-called "choice." The deck is stacked against equity and community. The new structure is devoted only to the power of free enterprise.

It is still too early to know the longer-term impacts on New Orleans' children. Undoubtedly, some charter schools will soar. They'll become darlings of philanthropic donors and will have long waiting lists of students. Just as assuredly, many will fail. Nationally, the achievement results of charter schools have not been strong, as the other chapters in this book show.

By what criteria will the entrepreneurial segment of the charter school movement judge their success? What if schools become even more segregated—not just by race or income but also by other, more subtle factors? What if the Recovery School District schools continue to be seen as the "dumping ground?" Will Louisiana taxpayers be pleased with the use of their public dollars in this new educational marketplace? Will the architects of the new system be satisfied, as long as some families have "choice?"

When will we reach a "defining moment in history" when community values—equity, access, public ownership, public purpose, and others—trump the value of individual choice as a strategy for building our public schools? Wouldn't *that* be lovely?

Epilogue, January 2008

The 2007-08 school year began in New Orleans with 85 schools for students. Of those, 43—more than half—are charter schools.

In May 2007, Robin Jarvis, the inaugural superintendent of the Recovery District Schools, resigned. In her place, the state Department of Education hired former Chicago and Philadelphia superintendent Paul Vallas to run the Recovery district. Vallas is a seasoned superintendent and has made significant strides in correcting some of the most egregious problems within the Recovery schools. Class sizes are down and buildings are being renovated. A new comprehensive plan calls for a return to traditional neighborhood schools, and for operational transparency and shared practices between the city's traditional and charter schools.

At the same time, troubling aspects of chartering are beginning to emerge. In September 2007, the governing board at Lafayette Academy ousted Mosaica Education as the school's management company, charging that Mosaica had failed to live up to its promises to align the school's curriculum with state standards, and to create Individualized Education Plans for disabled students, among other things. Over 20 teachers and 200 students had left the school after its inaugural year.[18]

On a broader scale, evidence is emerging that New Orleans charter schools, like a number of charter schools elsewhere, are failing to accept and/or to provide services to special needs students. The *Times-Picayune* reported[19] that towards the end of the 2006-07 school year, the city's charter schools had lower percentages of special education students than the average, and that the Recovery district was serving a disproportionate number of disabled students.

Concerns around "push-outs" at charter schools—where charters pressure parents to "voluntarily withdraw" their child and to enroll instead in a traditional public school—have increased. Anecdotal evidence has been compelling enough that a national public television documentary is being developed to look at the issue.

The assessment scores in New Orleans in 2007 were, as expected, mixed. Some charter schools did well, others did not, and overall more charters showed declines in their test scores than showed improvement. Meanwhile, students continue to flood back into the Big Easy, many with physical and psychological needs that make it crucial that the city's public education system serve them with fairness and purpose.

Can the market do that? The evidence so far clearly says no.

LEIGH DINGERSON IS THE EDUCATION TEAM LEADER AT THE CENTER FOR COMMUNITY CHANGE IN WASHINGTON, D.C., WHERE SHE HAS WORKED FOR A DECADE. SHE IS THE AUTHOR OF THE CENTER'S OCTOBER 2006 BOOKLET ON THE NEW ORLEANS SCHOOLS, *DISMANTLING A COMMUNITY*, AND IS EDITOR OF THE CENTER'S *EDUCATION ORGANIZING* NEWSLETTER, WHICH SHARES EFFORTS OF GRASSROOTS ORGANIZATIONS WORKING TO IMPROVE PUBLIC SCHOOLS. SHE HAS ALSO BEEN A COMMUNITY ORGANIZER WITH ACORN, WORKING IN TEXAS, ARKANSAS, AND SOUTH CAROLINA.

Endnotes

1. Goldberg, M., "Missing School in the Big Easy: As Kids in New Orleans Are Turned Away from Filled Schools, the City Gambles Its Future on Charter Schools," Salon.com, February 13, 2006.
2. Hill, P. T., "Re-creating Public Education in New Orleans," *Education Week*, September 21, 2005.
3. State of Louisiana, Executive Order No. KBB 2005-58 *"Emergency Suspensions to Assist in Meeting Educational Needs of Louisiana Students,"* retrieved from www.legis.state.la.us/katrina/eoorders/05-58.pdf on January 30, 2008.
4. Chapter 42, Charter School Demonstration Programs Law, retrieved from www.doe.state.la.us/lde/uploads/8384.doc on January 30, 2008.
5. Klein, N., *The Shock Doctrine: The Rise of Disaster Capitalism* (New York: Metropolitan Books, 2007) p. 17.
6. Maxwell, L. A., "Lawsuits Say Too Few Schools Open in New Orleans," *Education Week*, February 15, 2006.

7. Saulny, S., "Rough Start for State's Effort to Remake Faltering Schools in New Orleans," *New York Times*, August 21, 2006.
8. The "Knowledge Is Power Program" (KIPP) is a national franchise of charter schools that markets to low-income, African-American children.
9. Maryland State Department of Education, *An Evaluation of the Maryland Charter School Program*, October 2006; retrieved from www.marylandpublicschools.org/NR/rdolyres/1CEB8910-211A-47E0-909F C452B3A76CAB/11238/CSProgramEval.pdf on January 30, 2008.
10. "Education Secretary Announces Big Charter School Grant for Louisiana," Associated Press, June 13, 2006.
11. Ritea, S., "Recovery District to Delay Classes," *Times-Picayune*, June 14, 2006.
12. Email from Katherine Whitney, Chief of Staff for the Recovery School District, to Lance Hill, Tulane University, July 25, 2006.
13. Simon, D., and Ritea, S., "For Students on Waiting Lists Life Is Put on Hold," *Times-Picayune*, February 4, 2007.
14. In March 2007, Baptist Community Ministries announced a new $4.2 million initiative to provide support to the city's charter schools.
15. The TeachNOLA website has since been changed, but it continues to direct certified and uncertified teaching applicants to separate pages.
16. Algiers Charter School Association Employee Handbook, 2007-08, retrieved from www.algierscharterschools.org/downloads/2007/ACSA%20Handbook.doc on January 30, 2008. This information is on p. 20.
17. Waldman, A., "Reading, Writing, Resurrection," *Atlantic Monthly*, January/February 2007.
18. Simon, D., "Charter School Wins One Against Company" *Times-Picayune*, September 15, 2007.
19. Ritea, S., "Some Accuse New Orleans' East Bank Charter Schools of Turning Away Students with Special Needs," *Times-Picayune*, April 30, 2007.

Profits and Privatization:
The Ohio Experience
AMY HANAUER

In 1997, Ohio authorized a pilot project for charter schools in struggling urban districts. But what was sold to the public as an experimental innovation quickly blossomed into a privatization and for-profit dream come true, thanks largely to the political contributions of well-connected entrepreneurs. Within a decade, Ohio's charters grew from a pilot of 20 schools to an industry of 313 schools receiving more than $600 million annually in state and federal dollars and enrolling more than 75,000 students.[1] Charters have grown so quickly that in 2006-07, six Ohio cities had over 13 percent of their students enrolled in charter schools.[2]

Yet the academic performance of Ohio charter schools overall is dismal, and lags behind that of traditional public schools serving poor and minority students.

Perhaps more than any other of the 40 states with charter legislation, Ohio is a case study in *how not* to do charter schools. Some of the disturbing developments:

- More than half the state's charter money goes to for-profit companies whose bottom line is sometimes less the well-being of the children than the balance of their bank accounts. The largest and most-well known of the charter operators, White Hat Management, had only two of its 31 schools make the federal benchmark of "Adequate Yearly Progress" in 2006-07. Despite the questionable quality at many of its schools, White Hat made $4.16 million in profit during 2004-05.[3]
- Financial irregularities and questionable practices have been rampant. At nearly two dozen charter schools, records were missing and the books were in such disarray in 2006-07 that the state auditor deemed the schools "unauditable."
- Overall, 13 percent of the charters started between 1997 and 2006 were of such low quality that they had to be shut down.

Some of the failed charters left students stranded midyear or did not give teachers final paychecks. Before they were shut down, some schools went so far as to feign student disabilities in order to increase payments, operate without textbooks or toilet paper, or employ convicted felons as teachers and principals.

The situation is so disturbing that even charter school supporters are among those calling for increased accountability. "It's hard to defend a school that lasted less than three years and spent $5 million in state and federal money," Terry Ryan, a vice president overseeing Ohio education policy for the pro-charter Thomas B. Fordham Foundation based in Dayton, said after one Columbus charter was shut down.

Performance, For-profits, and Betrayed Promises

This essay reviews research on the academic performance of Ohio's charter schools, their accountability to the public, and their adherence to the original vision that charters were to be engines of innovation to help reform all public schools. The first section examines charter school performance on state tests as compared to traditional public schools as a whole, using the most recent data available, and to traditional public schools primarily serving low-income students and students of color, using slightly older data. The second section looks at the largest charter school operator in Ohio, White Hat Management, as an example of what happens when politically connected, for-profit entities take over a charter system. The third section summarizes several other charter school calamities, illustrating that while White Hat may be the largest charter operator, it is not alone in betraying the original vision of charter schools. The paper concludes with suggestions for a more accountable system. Drawing heavily on accounts from a variety of organizations—the *Cleveland Plain Dealer* and *Columbus Dispatch* newspapers; the Ohio Education Association; Policy Matters Ohio (the nonpartisan research institute where I am executive director), and the state's Legislative Office of Education Oversight—this essay finds substantial reason to rein in Ohio's unaccountable, for-profit charter school industry.

Noble Goals

Charter schools began in Ohio with the promise that they would deliver educational quality to troubled communities. As the pro-charter group US Charter Schools notes on its website, "The intention of most charter school legislation is to:

- "Increase opportunities for learning and access to quality education for all students.
- "Create choice for parents and students within the public school system.
- "Provide a system of accountability for results in public education.
- "Encourage innovative teaching practices.
- "Create new professional opportunities for teachers; Encourage community and parent involvement in public education.
- "Leverage improved public education broadly ...

"Parents and teachers choose charter schools primarily for educational reasons—high academic standards, small class size, innovative approaches, or educational philosophies in line with their own."[4]

Reality is not always in line with intentions, however. In Ohio, the largely for-profit charter industry has rarely delivered the elusive goals outlined by US Charter Schools. A handful of excellent charters shine, but they are exceptions. For the average charter school in Ohio, standards, if measured by test score achievement, have been lower. Accountability, whether in performance or in financial spending, has been inadequate. Class sizes have been larger in many schools. Innovation, if it exists, is not disseminated to other schools, as Ohio charter sponsors typically reveal little about what they spend and how. And educational quality among charters as a whole is poor.

Performance Problems

Charter legislation passed in Ohio at a time when parents and students had good reason to be frustrated with the outcomes at big, urban districts. Charters started, and remain concentrated, in such districts. However, 11 years after legislators decided to begin this experiment, charter schools in Ohio include many dismal failures. Overall, the charter record is unimpressive at best, when measured by the most recent state performance tests.

For schools that issued report cards in 2007, about two-thirds of public schools made Adequate Yearly Progress, compared to just a third of charter schools (an improvement over the previous year for charter schools.)

Ohio charter schools drastically lag behind traditional public schools in other ways. Only 8 percent of charters received a rating of excellent or effective, compared to 63 percent of public schools. More than two-thirds of charter schools (43 percent) received a rating of academic watch or academic emergency, compared to just 11 percent of traditional schools. Furthermore, more than a quarter of charter schools were not rated, compared to less than 10 percent of public schools (see Figure A).

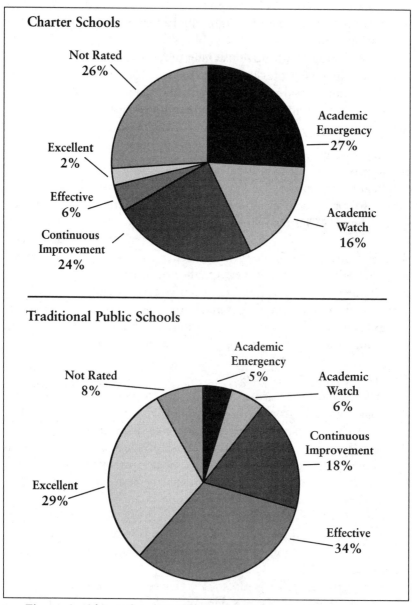

Figure A: Ohio School Performance Report Cards
Source: Ohio Department of Education, 2006-07 report cards

Many education researchers raise excellent questions about state tests and their validity for assessing performance.[5] That said, the performance tests described in this section remain the simplest way to assess school quality. Public schools are judged by these standards and the charter industry in Ohio was justified in part by assertions that urban districts were failing by just this sort of accountability measure. These tests are a blunt tool, but they are the only comparison available. They reveal poor, if rising, performance for charters.[6]

The small number of charter schools rated excellent in 2006-07 includes three district-sponsored schools, one school for gifted students, and one for children with autism. All are nonprofit and are hardly typical of the for-profit model that constitutes so much of the charter school industry in Ohio.

Ohio charter schools are concentrated in poor urban districts and have students who are more disadvantaged than public school students statewide, making comparisons like those above less than entirely fair. That said, Ohio charter students are not, as a whole, quite as disadvantaged economically and linguistically as students in Ohio's urban districts, although they are more likely to be African-American.

Both Ohio's urban schools and the state's charter schools have solid majorities that are poor and African-American and only small numbers that are Hispanic. But the Ohio Education Association found in a 2006 report on charter schools that while charter school students were more likely to be African-American, students in the state's eight large urban districts were more likely to be economically disadvantaged, nearly twice as likely to be Hispanic, much more likely to be of limited English proficiency, and substantially more likely to have a disability.[7]

Research from the 2004-05 school year compared charter schools to traditional public schools serving more similar student populations. The study, conducted by the Ohio Education Association's Andy Jewell, compared proficiency test scores in charter and traditional schools for economically disadvantaged students and for African-American students.[8] (Charter school performance on state tests has improved slightly since the time of this analysis.)

The Public School Performance Advantage

Across 21 different test results for seven grade levels, Jewell found that traditional school students from economically disadvantaged backgrounds had consistently and dramatically higher scores on every test. Considering all scores together, public school students averaged 19.3 points higher than charter students from similar economic backgrounds.[9] A similar public school advantage was found when controlling for race. African-American students in traditional public schools consistently performed better than black students at charter schools in Ohio in the 2004-05 school year, with better performance on every one of the 21 tests. Combining all tests, the study found a 13.1 point public school advantage.[10] Public schools also do a better job of assessing more of their students. In 2004-05, charter schools had 45 of the 50 lowest participation rates on math tests and 47 of the 50 lowest participation rates among reading tests.[11]

Although charters don't out-perform traditional public schools, the way they are funded hurts district's funding. The Cleveland public school system lost more than $82 million to charters in FY 2007,[12] and the Dayton public school system lost almost 21 percent of its funding to private charters in 2005.[13] Enrollment in Ohio's eight urban districts dropped from 305,516 in the 1997-98 school year to 228,058 in the 2006-07 school year, according to state enrollment data.

An Egregious Case

While the data shows a struggling system, individual stories reveal reasons why the state hasn't seized control of this industry. There is perhaps no better example in the entire country of the problems with for-profit charters than White Hat Management.

White Hat is owned and operated by Akron businessman and lobbyist extraordinaire David Brennan, who sports a white hat to bolster his cowboy-like image. Brennan started his education entrepreneurial career by starting publicly funded, private voucher schools, and jumped into charters by founding White Hat in 1998. By 2007, White Hat claimed more than 9,500 students at 31 schools in Ohio. It raked in more than $79 million dollars in state, federal, and local funds last year, according to data from the Ohio Department of Education and from White Hat's web site.

Although White Hat's numbers—enrollment, number of schools, and state funds—are down from peak levels several years ago, the company still has ambitious plans.[14] Its website boasts that "White Hat currently operates schools in Arizona, Colorado, Florida, Michigan, Ohio and Pennsylvania. Future schools will be built in Texas, New Mexico, Indiana, New York and other states across the U.S." Overall, it purports to be the third largest operator of K-12 charter schools in the country.[15]

While evidence indicates that White Hat Management skimps on educational services, its website shows the public relations benefit of spending money on promotion. To look at the website, White Hat is, as the name tries to imply, a long-awaited champion for those seeking better schools. As the homepage boasts: "Think of us as a company dedicated to students reaching their full potential. White Hat looks at problems, comes up with solutions and provides proven results."

The website's glowing rhetoric is belied by White Hat's operations in Ohio, however. And the lack of accountability in Brennan's education empire is emblematic of what can happen when a potentially creative reform is captured by those who stand to profit financially or who have little regard for public oversight.

Brennan established his relationships the old-fashioned way: he gave enormous campaign contributions. He personally gave more than $120,000 to, and raised more than $500,000 more for, former Ohio Governor George Voinovich, a Republican who was instrumental in the privatization of schools in Ohio. He also gave hundreds of thousands of dollars to the Ohio Republican Party and its candidates.[16]

Brennan also connected other wealthy donors with politicians. For example, he held a $25,000-per-person backyard fundraiser for Voinovich, where attendees could rub noses with the first President Bush. This generosity undoubtedly helped sway Voinovich, whom Brennan once called "a hard sell ... a tough convert" on school choice.[17]

But although some politicians were tough converts and Brennan had to make substantial campaign contributions, it paid off. Gov. Voinovich named Brennan chair of the state's Commission on Educational Choice, which allowed Brennan to craft state policy toward using public taxpayers' dollars to build privately owned for-profit schools.

By 2005, White Hat had received more than $400 million in Ohio taxpayer dollars.[18] But the dollars did not necessarily mean Brennan was open to public accountability. When the *Cleveland Plain Dealer* did an extensive series on charter schools, Brennan refused to be interviewed or to answer most written questions. Equally troubling, his schools have done their best to keep financial and performance details quiet.

Brennan's charter school empire includes Hope Academies, which has one Cleveland high school but primarily instructs K-8 students; Life Skills Centers, aimed at high school-age students who are at risk for dropping out or have done so; and Alternative Education Academy (AEA), an online K-12 school operating across Ohio. The exact financial relationships between White Hat and its schools are often unclear, but what is known is that White Hat is in the driver's seat. The Hope Academy schools, for instance, cede 96 percent of the public dollars they get to White Hat.[19]

Although parents are supposed to be able to hold charters accountable, White Hat usually holds school meetings on weekday mornings when few working parents can attend. Predictably, few parents ever do. Still, Brennan claims to have parental interests at heart. "I trust parents," the *Columbus Dispatch* quoted Brennan as saying. "I've learned to trust that unemployed, prostitute, minority mother more than any educrat I've ever met in my life."[20] If meetings are not made easily accessible to parents (be they "unemployed prostitutes" or not) White Hat works hard to accommodate board members: Hope Academy board members are given laptop computers and paid up to $55,000 a year, exceeding most teacher salaries. Meanwhile, at all but two White Hat schools, the average teacher salaries were less than $35,000 a year in 2006-07, according to the Ohio Department of Education.

Following the corporate model, White Hat has been known for interlocking Board relationships among its schools. Until stricter laws reined in the practice, 15 of White Hat's 18 Cuyahoga and Summit County schools had four overlapping board members, none of whom were educators.[21]

Limited Financial Reporting

Even though it depends on public tax dollars ($100 million in state funding in the 2005 fiscal year, for instance),[22] White Hat severely limits how much financial information it releases to the public. White Hat schools comply with Ohio law, but the requirements have been shamefully lax, making it impossible to assess spending.[23] In 2005, for instance, the company failed to report what it spent on teaching: Instruction costs were lumped in with administration, building operations, and other expenses. White Hat also did not disclose what it spent on textbooks.

A large portion of White Hat's expenses at its schools went to a general "overhead" or "purchased services" category. At the Life

Skills schools run by White Hat, this category accounted for nearly half of all spending, leaving unclear how money is spent overall on the schools versus how much the parent company is profiting. After legislative and rule changes required more disclosure, for the first time White Hat reported its expenses at each of the schools it operates for the fiscal year 2005. Based on those audit reports, White Hat appeared to have earned $4.16 million on revenues of $116.95 million in its Ohio schools during the 2004-05 school year. Every Life Skills school was profitable and three produced more in earnings than was paid in salaries. Each Hope Academy reported that White Hat spent more than the revenue it took in, while the company was modestly profitable at its online, statewide Alternative Education Academy.

However, the massive overhead expenditures make this description incomplete. At Life Skills schools, the accurate story is particularly unclear. White Hat could be having its own subsidiaries provide services it reports as overhead, resulting in large additional profits beyond what can be discerned from financial statements. Profit size simply can't be determined from this vague reporting.

Beyond substantial overhead spending, the White Hat schools spend significantly on contract services, including professional, technical, and property services. Nearly half (48.3 percent) of all Life Skills spending of $51.4 million is on either overhead or contracted services. No further breakout of this spending is available. In contrast, traditional public schools spend a much larger share of their budgets on salaries and employee benefits and report clearly how much goes to different categories.

White Hat schools collectively reported to the Ohio Department of Education that all but $169,745 of their $122.6 million in 2004-05 expenditures went into administrative spending. In three financial reports filed by White Hat-operated schools, long strings of zeroes describe how much was spent for guidance, health, fiscal services, treatment for students with disabilities, and other categories. These are all items that traditional public schools report on clearly.[24]

The federal Internal Revenue Service (IRS), meanwhile, has questioned the contracts between White Hat Management and its various schools. It has raised concerns about whether contracts with White Hat were "one-sided" and designed for the benefit of White Hat, noting that elements of the contracts were "completely arbitrary" and "not in the best interests" of the schools. The IRS also questions advertising expenditures, equipment purchases, interest purchases, equipment ownership, and other issues.[25]

In short, the IRS found evidence that Ohio officials were willfully ignoring that White Hat was running itself as a ruthless, for-profit company, to the detriment of both the schools and the students in them.

Poor Performance

The paltry financial reporting doesn't serve the public well, and neither, so far, has White Hat's performance.

In 2006-07, 10 of White Hat's 18 Life Skills Center were on Academic Emergency while the others were on Academic Watch. (This was an improvement from the previous school year, when all 17 of the rated Life Skills schools were in Academic Emergency.) Results for the Hope Academies are better, with five rated Continuous Improvement, seven on Academic Watch, and one on Academic Emergency.

In all, only two of the 31 White Hat schools listed made Adequate Yearly Progress for 2006-07, the same number that made the benchmark the year before.

The weak performance is partly due to a less qualified and more financially stressed teaching staff. In addition to the low salaries at White Hat, Life Skills Center of Lake Erie had more than 20 percent of its classes taught by a teacher who was not rated "highly qualified" and Life Skills of North Akron had more than a quarter of its classes taught by a teacher not deemed "highly qualified."[26]

Who Profits?

Although much financial information about Ohio's charter schools is clouded in confusion, one thing is clear. More than half of the state's charter money goes to for-profit companies.[27] Even when Hope schools were initially applying for state funding, education department officials noticed that teacher salaries were startlingly low, student-teacher ratios alarmingly high (30-to-1), and company-projected profits steadily growing.

White Hat Management has also been adept at making side deals that save it money, leaving more tax dollars available to be funneled into profits. The Cleveland Catholic Diocese, for instance, gave White Hat Management bargain basement rent for the use of empty Catholic schools—but those real estate savings were not used to support services for students. Instead, White Hat Management

turned around and charged its individual schools using those buildings a total of $1.5 million more than White Hat Management was
paying to the Diocese for rent.

What's more, because the school buildings are owned by the
church, there is no property tax on the buildings. Thus White Hat
Management, a for-profit concern, is avoiding about $700,000 in
local taxes.[28]

Real-estate deals are not the only way in which White Hat uses
"creative" practices to further bolster its profit balance. When individual White Hat schools have insufficient funds, they often borrow
from White Hat Management at an extremely high 10 percent interest rate.[29]

According to a multistate study by the Evaluation Center at
Western Michigan University, the for-profit model that has dominated in Ohio has had negative educational effects elsewhere as
well. The study found that states dominated by profit-making companies have seen poor charter performance, weak charter accountability, and little progress over time.[30]

As the *New York Times* editorialized in response to the study:
"To salvage the charter movement, the states will need to abandon
the strategy, now discredited, that consists largely of giving public
money to what are basically private schools and then looking the
other way."[31]

Political Maneuvering

Brennan's political fundraising for Republicans, on its own, raises
troubling questions. But the *Cleveland Plain Dealer* newspaper has
chronicled more disturbing crossing of lines.

Take, for instance, the career of Sally Perz, the Republican who
sponsored Ohio's initial charter school legislation.

Perz left political office to become a lobbyist for the University
of Toledo, where she was a member of the university's Charter
School Council. This council approved White Hat's proposal for a
statewide virtual (online) charter school, for which the school
received $32 million in taxpayer money. Perz's daughter, Allison,
later formed a nonprofit that became the Ohio Council of Community Schools. Sally Perz, who had moved on to become a private
consultant, was paid $61,200 from her daughter's agency in the first
year, and was also paid by White Hat Management as a lobbyist.
Later, 19 White Hat schools hired the Ohio Council of Community
Schools as their sponsor, paying it $405,000. Four other firms hired

Sally Perz as a lobbyist and hired Allison's organization as their sponsor.[32] These cozy relationships may help explain the weak oversight that for-profit charters have received in Ohio.

Not an Isolated Example

While White Hat schools' practices are troubling, other for-profit charters in Ohio have provided similar examples of poor education, terrible accountability, and money that went either to profits or disappeared. As of last school year, 47 charter schools had shut down in Ohio, 13 percent of those that had opened.[33] According to the *Columbus Dispatch*, "many were left in financial ruin." Each year, some that are still open are designated "unauditable."

Take the case of Harte Crossroads. A set of two single-sex academies in Columbus, Harte Crossroads spent about $5 million in state and federal money but closed midyear after less than three years in operation. Over 200 students were left stranded, with missing transcripts and limited ability to transition to new schools. As the *Columbus Dispatch* wrote, "They opened in fall 2004 with no permanent building, no textbooks, and plenty of chaos ... now, only one thing lives on: debt."[34]

That debt has now been tallied at more than $1 million owed to state, federal, and local government, and $2.66 million to 188 creditors, including teachers who hadn't been paid.[35]

Ryan, the vice president from the Dayton-based Fordham Foundation, lamented the effect of such charter failures on the overall movement. "These high-profile, very expensive scandals ... it's hard," he told the *Columbus Dispatch*. "It's a weight on (the charter-school movement). It's an anchor."

As the *Columbus Dispatch* noted, it's also hard on the students, 77 of whom still hadn't re-enrolled in any school in Columbus nearly a year after the charter's closure.

Derrick Smith, a former student at one of the Harte Crossroads schools, told the *Columbus Dispatch* he had no record of the classes he'd taken, and that the school had been in disarray. "They didn't have everything situated," he said. "We had no teachers. The computers didn't work."

Even the school's founder and operator, Anita Nelam, was quoted in the *Columbus Dispatch* saying, "The whole thing is just one big tragedy on so many levels."

The *Columbus Dispatch* has also reported on large payments to online cyberschools for education that never got delivered. In September

2000, according to a *Dispatch* account, the cyberschool eCot received $932,030 for 2,270 students, but could provide evidence that only seven students had logged on. The next month, the school got another $983,750 for 2,346 students but could prove only 506 logins. In fact, of the students at eCot, by the end of that month only 25 percent had computers. Although a state investigation uncovered this problem, the state had no power to demand a refund, because guidelines were so weak.[36]

More than five years later, similar problems remained. A *Columbus Dispatch* editorial in February 2007 lamented the degree to which virtual students continue to attend virtual schools. Eleven online schools have earned state investigations for reporting 100 percent attendance despite having many students that rarely logged on. Lucas County Educational Service Center, eCot's sponsor, found that the school had technology problems (with students unable to consistently access materials), inventory issues, and unacceptable student-to-teacher ratios, possibly as high as 150 to 170 students per teacher.[37]

For a long time, Ohio's reluctance to shut down terrible charters only made the situation worse. The International Preparatory School in Cleveland failed to ever meet a single state academic benchmark, yet limped along for six years, overestimating enrollment and getting state funding.[38] The operator of the Cleveland Academy of Math, Science and Technology bilked the state out of $1.3 million for running the appealing-sounding charter school. The academy routinely billed the state for 681 students but never had more than 128 kids, according to federal charges. The school was paid $5,821 per student in its final year, and engaged in dishonest behavior related to rent, building purchase, building renovation, and building sales.[39]

The entertainingly named High Life Youth Development Center in Columbus, meanwhile, closed in 2000 after just six months. It had received $257,000 for students who never showed up, accumulating $650,000 in debt, and spending $331,000 on administrator salaries and only $106,000 on regular instruction. Another Columbus High Life school closed with nearly $2 million in debt. And the list goes on—feigning student disabilities to increase payments, running schools without textbooks or toilet paper, employing convicted felons as teachers and principals, claiming nonexistent students, and more.[40]

While the state was slow to close charters no matter how egregious their behavior, legislators did punish those who tried to assess charter schools. After Ohio's Legislative Office of Education Oversight produced one too many studies raising careful questions about charter schools, the office was shut down. The closure reduced even further what had been limited official capacity to assess charters.

With new political leadership in Ohio, the friendly attitude toward questionable and for-profit charters is changing. Democrat Ted Strickland took office as governor in 2007, a reflection of the transitional political climate in the state. In line with this new climate, Attorney General Mark Dann is suing four charter schools. One is the New Choices Community School, which has met just one of 29 academic benchmarks in six years of operation. Another is the Colin Powell Leadership Academy, which has met one of 61 benchmarks in the same period.[41] Together, these two schools in Dayton have received more than $17 million from the state. In early 2008, Dann filed suit against Harmony Community School in Cincinnati, citing almost 600 pages of evidence that chronicle what Dann called "abject academic failure, gross financial mismanagement, ethical lapses, and what amounts to consumer fraud."[42]

Conclusion

Ohio's public school system faces very real and daunting problems. The school funding system was found to be unconstitutional over a decade ago, and funding and outcomes vary widely by district. Performance at urban schools has been inching upward, but graduation rates in urban districts remain dismal. Students in poor districts are highly mobile—many switch schools frequently throughout their education, sometimes midyear. Skills slide backward each summer, requiring substantial catch-up time in the fall. Even for students who graduate from poor districts, transition to higher education or jobs is often rocky.

Charter schools were brought to Ohio as a response to these challenges. And a handful of highly respected charter schools—usually independent, community-based charters—are rising to the challenge. As a whole, however, the charter school industry has failed to even remotely deliver on its promises. There is more to be learned from Ohio's high-performing traditional public schools than from the vast majority of extremely unsuccessful charter schools that typify the industry. Accountability, innovation, high performance, teacher quality—these can be found in traditional public schools in Ohio. And they should be the norm in every school.

Policy makers and educators should turn their attention to understanding and replicating the best in Ohio's traditional public schools, and should turn their back on the failed for-profit charter industry that has been at best a distraction and at worst a terrible failure. Ohio students deserve the accountability, performance, equity, and quality that is best found in truly public schools.

Author's note: I'm grateful to the Open Society Institute, George Wood, Piet van Lier, and Zach Schiller. As always, I thank Mark, Max, and Katrina Cassell.

AMY HANAUER IS THE FOUNDING EXECUTIVE DIRECTOR OF POLICY MATTERS OHIO, A NONPROFIT, NONPARTISAN RESEARCH INSTITUTE FOCUSING ON POLICY ISSUES OF IMPORTANCE TO WORKING FAMILIES. HANAUER HAS A MASTER'S OF PUBLIC ADMINISTRATION FROM THE UNIVERSITY OF WISCONSIN-MADISON AND HAS PREVIOUSLY DONE RESEARCH AND POLICY WORK IN WISCONSIN, COLORADO, AND WASHINGTON, D.C. HANAUER ALSO IS ON THE BOARD OF THE NEW YORK-BASED ORGANIZATION DEMOS, AN ADVOCACY AND RESEARCH GROUP DEDICATED TO A VIBRANT, INCLUSIVE DEMOCRACY, AND ON THE NATIONAL ADVISORY COMMITTEE TO THE ECONOMIC ANALYSIS AND RESEARCH NETWORK AT THE ECONOMIC POLICY INSTITUTE BASED IN WASHINGTON, D.C.

Appendix I
Charter Legislative History—Expansion without Results

The charter school movement was begun as an experiment in Ohio, in 1997, to see if freedom from some regulations could deliver better student performance.[43] After allowing an initial 20 schools as a pilot project, the state steadily added to the number and geographic reach of charters, while adding little increased accountability. In the past year, led by an aggressive attorney general and a more critical governor, some long-overdue but too-modest accountability measures have been enacted.

Table A shows the legislative history of Ohio charter schools.

Year	Action	Description
1997	HB 215	Established a five-year charter school pilot study in Lucas County, Ohio, limited new independent charter schools to 20, and permitted an unlimited number of conversion schools by districts.
1997	SB 55	Before any charters had opened, extended permission for independent charter schools to other cities in Ohio's big eight districts (Akron, Canton, Cincinnati, Cleveland, Columbus, Dayton, and Youngstown); allowed state Board of Education to be a sponsoring entity for new charters.
1999	HB 282	Allowed charters in any of Ohio's 21 largest urban districts and in other districts labeled as in academic emergency; ended pilot program.
2003	HB 364	Added Academic Watch districts to those where independent charters can be sited; capped number of charter schools at 225; reduced oversight role of Ohio Board of Education.
2003	HB 3	Reduced permissible sites for new independent charters back to the big eight, unless a charter was already in existence in another location.
2005	HB 66	Capped new independent charters at 30, restricted district-sponsored new charters to an additional 30, forbade new internet charter schools until standards are established; required achievement standards for charters and sanctions for failing charters. Later delayed by HB 530.
2007	HB 79	Schools rated academic emergency or "F" for three years must be closed at end of current school year; schools deemed "unauditable" will lose state aid; higher standards for sponsors; more oversight for education department; penalties for failure to report performance data.

Table A: History of Action on Charter Schools in Ohio
Sources: Ohio legislative website, interviews,[44] OEA 2006 Charter School Report

Endnotes

1. According to the Ohio Department of Education website at www.ode.state.oh.us there were 77,000 Ohio students enrolled in 313 "community" or charter schools in 2006-07, receiving $530.8 million in state dollars, $78.2 million in consolidated federal funds and $17.5 million in multiyear federal grants.

2. National Alliance for Public Charter Schools, "Public Charter Schools Increase Market Share and Raise Student Academic Achievement," October 17, 2007.

3. Schiller, Z., "Limited Accountability: Financial Reporting at White Hat Charter Schools," *Policy Matters Ohio*, October 2006, p. 4.

4. Benefits description at www.uscharterschools.org/pub/uscs_docs/o/index.htm.

5. For more about the limits of these tests and the concerns being raised about them, see the Forum for Education and Democracy at www.forumforeducation.org/.

6. Ohio Department of Education, "2006-07 Community Schools Annual Governor's Report," retrieved from www.ode.state.oh.us/GD/Templates/Pages/ODE/ODEDetail.aspx?page=3&TopicRelationID=662&ContentID=41601&Content=41601 on January 29, 2008.

7. Ohio Education Association, "Ohio's Charter Schools Program," 2007.

8. Jewell, A., "Ohio Education Association, 2006", pp. 13-14. The 2006 report was based on 2004-05 report card data.

9. Jewell, p. 16.

10. Jewell, p. 17.

11. As quoted in Klupinski, S., "Experience, Knowledge Not Required," *Catalyst Cleveland*, May 2005.

12. Ohio Department of Education, "2006-07 Community Schools Annual Governor's Report."

13. *Cleveland Plain Dealer*, March 21, 2006.

14. Livingston, S., Stephens, S., and Paynter, B., "Who's Profiting from Ohio's Charter Schools?" *Cleveland Plain Dealer*, March 19, 2006.

15. www.whitehatmgmt.com.

16. Livingston, Stephens, and Paynter, March 19, 2006.

17. Hallett, J., "Self-appointed Superintendent Industrialist Builds Ninth-largest School District Using Political Clout," *Columbus Dispatch*, October 23, 2005.

18. Livingston, Stephens, and Paynter, March 19, 2006, and Ohio Department of Education, January 2008.

19. Livingston, Stephens and Paynter, March 19, 2006.

20. Hallett, October 25, 2005.

21. Livingston, Stephens, and Paynter, March 19, 2006, and March 21, 2006.

22. Schiller, Z., October 2006.

23. ibid, available at www.policymattersohio.org/limitedaccountability_2006.htm.

24. Schiller, Z., October 2006, p. 14, quoting the 4,502 statements schools are required to provide to the Ohio Department of Education, for Riverside Academy, Life Skills Center of Akron, and Hope Academy Broadway Campus.

25. Livingston, Stephens, and Paynter, March 19, 2006.
26. Ohio Department of Education report card data at www.ode.state.oh.us.
27. Livingston, Stephens, and Paynter, March 19, 2006.
28. ibid.
29. *Cleveland Plain Dealer*, March 21, 2006.
30. "Reining in Charter Schools," *New York Times* editorial, May 10, 2006
31. ibid.
32. "Who's Minding the Store," *Cleveland Plain Dealer*, March 19, 2006.
33. Smith Richards, J., "Dead Schools Debt Mounts, Tally Stands at $1.6 Million; Students' Fates Uncertain," *Columbus Dispatch*, April 1, 2007.
34. Smith Richards, J. April 1, 2007.
35. Smith Richards, J. "Closed Charter Schools' Mess Lingers, Harte Crossroads Owes Millions, Report Says," *Columbus Dispatch*, January 10, 2008.
36. Williams, S., "Coming Your Way: Cyberschools: This Newest Wrinkle in Privatization Is Being Marketed to Christian Home-schoolers," *Rethinking Schools,* Summer 2002.
37. Klupinski, S., "Shape Up or Ship Out in Lucas County," *Catalyst Cleveland*, May 2005, p. 9.
38. *Cleveland Plain Dealer*, March 19, 2006.
39. ibid.
40. Martin, D. W., "Bad Apples: When a Disgraced Westlake High School Principal Resurfaced at a Charter School, He Revealed an Education Experiment Gone Awry," *Scene Magazine*, September 3, 2003.
41. Candisky, C., "Closings Sought: Dann Sues 2 Charter Schools, Dayton Schools Accused of Betraying Standards," *Columbus Dispatch*, September 13, 2007.
42. Office of the Attorney General, "Attorney General Dann Files Fourth Charter School Suit: Says Harmony Community School, in Cincinnati, Must Be Held Accountable for Academic, Financial, Ethical Failures," retrieved from www.ag.state.oh.us/press/08/01/pr080118.asp on January 18, 2008.
43. Legislative Office of Education Oversight, "The Operating Costs of Ohio eCommunity Schools," June 2005, at www.loeo.state.oh.us/reports/PreEleSecPDF/eSchools2_Web.pdf.
44. Interview with George Boas, who had been chief of staff for Ohio State Senator C.J. Prentiss, a member of the Senate education committee, during much of this time period.

"Evolution" or Destruction?
A Look at Washington, D.C.
BY ZEIN EL-AMINE AND LEE GLAZER

On a winter evening in 2006, members of the Save Our Schools coalition attended a community meeting to discuss the fate of the shuttered Bruce School in the rapidly gentrifying Columbia Heights neighborhood of Washington, D.C. The coalition of parents, teachers, trade unionists, and community activists that we had helped found had spent the previous year fighting the sale of public property, educating school communities about the negative effects of privatization, and demonstrating, lobbying, and testifying about the need to fund public school modernizations. Although the school system no longer needed its entire inventory of buildings, Save Our Schools argued that the city had an obligation to maintain public property for public use. That evening, teachers and parents had come up with the perfect use for the vacant building: there were three schools in the vicinity of Bruce that needed renovating, so the school could serve as a swing space during construction.

Conditions were favorable, since the efforts of Save Our Schools and other community activists had convinced the City Council to modernize the traditional public schools. But charter school lobbyists had mobilized their forces as well and came to the meeting with students and parents to make their case for them. After several students spoke, a leading charter school lobbyist summed up their position. Charter schools, she said, are "the evolution of public education."[1] The Darwinian rhetoric implied an inevitable and natural outcome: it is pointless to renovate traditional public schools because they are fundamentally moribund.

At the same meeting, a principal at one of the neighboring public schools pleaded to use Bruce School as swing space; her school, she explained, was literally without walls. At a follow-up meeting with the ward council member, public school teachers and parents in Save Our Schools made their case again. The council member, whose office is decorated with shovels he'd received at groundbreakings for new condominiums and stores in his ward, explained that he was under tremendous pressure from developers and lobbyists to "starve the beast," an unmistakable reference to public institutions. He added that the charter school movement was "bringing resources to the table"—meaning private funds.

Some months later, the city turned over the vacant Bruce School to César Chavez Public Charter School. The public schools, meanwhile, remain in a state of disrepair.

This was a pivotal moment in our growing understanding of privatization. We learned about the far-reaching influence of the charter school movement, its sizable behind-the-scenes resources, and its antagonism toward the traditional public school system. Most important, we learned to put the privatization of education in context— part of the "starving the beast" policies pushed by right-wing strategists and implemented by liberal politicians in urban centers to defund publicly funded services targeted at low- and moderate-income people.

Charter schools, introduced in the 1990s as "laboratories of innovation," have become instead laboratories for privatization. Nowhere is this more evident than in the nation's capital, where the experiments have been unchecked by local officials and have harmed, perhaps irreparably, the D.C. public schools.

Why Washington, D.C.?

Because Washington, D.C., lacks full representation in Congress, it is an ideal venue for social, economic, and educational experimentation. Congress limits the autonomy of locally elected officials and regularly meddles in local affairs. This has inhibited the development of a community-based civic culture and has allowed ideologically driven foundations and individuals to bypass the residents of D.C. and impose legislation without obtaining popular support.

D.C. charter schools were created by an act of Congress, the District of Columbia School Reform Act of 1995, and originally were seen as a compromise preventing private school vouchers.[2] (After George W. Bush's administration came to power, Congress, with the complicity of the mayor and elected school board president, mandated vouchers even though a Zogby poll showed that 85 percent of African-American voters and 76 percent of all voters opposed them.[3])

The School Reform Act, widely considered one of the most aggressive charter school laws in the nation, created two chartering boards that could issue up to 20 new charters a year and approve an unlimited number of "expansion" campuses under which existing charters expand by opening additional schools at a new site. The law, which Congress has amended several times, also mandates a per-pupil funding formula and additional money for facilities, and gives charters right of first offer and a 25 percent discount on surplus public property. The law also prohibits the imposition of neighborhood boundaries around charter schools.[4]

Public education in the nation's capital has been under assault since legalized forced segregation was ended in 1954. The promise of integration was never fully realized, however. White flight in the 1950s and 1960s, followed by middle-class black flight a decade later, left public schools with a majority population of low-income children of color. According to the 2005 census, Washington has a child poverty rate of 32 percent—the highest in the nation.[5] This demographic reality has been accompanied by a long process of underfunding and outright neglect of schools and other basic social rights, from affordable housing to child care and medical services. The result has been a downward spiral of political disenfranchisement and community atomization, a domestic version of the structural adjustment policies of the World Bank and International Monetary Fund under which loans to developing nations are tied to implementing free-market programs and privatizing publicly owned resources.

In D.C., this approach to economic development has displaced entire communities through outright demolition of affordable housing and, more insidiously, through the closure and repurposing of neighborhood public schools. Perhaps the best example of this is the redevelopment of the D.C. waterfront, an ongoing project that will culminate with the 2008 opening of an $800 million, publicly funded baseball stadium.

The redevelopment included the demolition of more than 1,100 public housing units[6] and the closing of several local public schools. One of them, the Giddings School, is now under long-term lease to Results, a private gym. The shuttered Syphax School was redeveloped as "affordable housing," where a two-bedroom unit listed for $285,000 in 2004. Parents at Van Ness Elementary successfully fought off efforts by a charter school to take over the building, only to have their school closed two years later due to declining enrollment.

Problems within the public school system have given the aura of legitimacy to privatization. Since 1996, the district has had seven superintendents and three mayoral takeover attempts. The Board of Education has been reconfigured four times. The Washington Teachers Union, meanwhile, has a history of ineffective leadership and corruption, culminating in the 2003 imprisonment of a former president. Even worse, the union leadership has ignored the needs of children and countenanced weak instructional leaders and incompetent teachers.

Add to this the outsourcing of special education and skilled labor, the reduction of custodial staff, deferred facilities modernization, and unfunded teacher pay raises, and one can better understand the havoc within the public school system. Although national politicians and the local media portray D.C. public schools as lavishly funded, the average per-pupil expenditure of $8,200 in 2007 is roughly equivalent to or less than surrounding suburban districts.[7] What's more, the amount that reaches D.C. classrooms is sometimes less than half the allocated amount, since in addition to paying for central office functions, around 20 percent of the district's budget goes to special education transportation and private placements. When charter schools presented themselves as "laboratories of reform," they appealed to a population whose confidence in the public schools was low.

Congress has made matters worse. When D.C. was teetering on the edge of insolvency in 1996, Congress forced the city to cede much of its home rule authority to a Control Board, which removed the superintendent of schools and all members of the elected Board of Education (the city's first popularly elected body). The Control Board then named a retired U.S. Army general to oversee the schools, established an appointed Emergency Board of Trustees, and handed over facilities management to the Army Corps of Engineers—which did no better with the district's school buildings than with the levees of New Orleans.

This was the political context in which charter schools appeared on the scene. With the election of Mayor Anthony Williams in 1998, who ceded the field to well-funded foundations and lobbyists, the charter movement gained momentum.

When the first charters opened in 1997, there were three schools enrolling a total of approximately 300 students. When Williams left office at the end of 2006, there were 66 charter school campuses enrolling 19,600 students.[8] A former member of the Control Board, Williams brought fiscal credibility to D.C. through a combination of trickle-down economics and structural adjustment. Partnering with the Federal City Council, a business group created in 1954 by *Washington Post* owner Philip Graham that functions as a shadow government representing regional corporate interests, Williams embarked on a program of privatization and gentrification that included the closure of the highly rated but underfunded D.C. General Hospital,[9] radical cuts in social services, the sale of public property, and the promotion of both charter schools and vouchers. Williams' mantra of attracting 100,000 new residents to a city "open for business" resulted in the highest income inequality in the nation, the lowest life expectancy, and the highest percentage of charter schools per capita—until Hurricane Katrina washed away the public school system in New Orleans.[10]

Charter Proliferation

In October 2007, around 22,000 students, nearly 30 percent of the city's total public school enrollment, attended one of the city's 87 charter school campuses.[11] Public officials have encouraged charter proliferation despite abysmal academic results, and their reluctance to acknowledge the lack of quality is related both to the congressionally mandated nature of D.C. charters and to the lack of an education plan by local officials. Every time a new charter school opens, students and resources leave the public schools, programs and teachers are cut, and the stage is set for another exodus the following year.

Even the loss of just five or six students can be devastating to a local school. Schools are funded on a per-pupil basis and in working out a local school budget, the district requires allocating $70,000 for each full-time teacher even though the actual salary is significantly lower for more junior faculty. Thus a loss of only a few students in one grade is enough to eliminate a full-time position. If enrollment dips too much, regardless of the reasons, closure is recommended. In 2006, for instance, Fletcher Johnson Educational Center was one of six public schools closed for underutilization of space. Rampant neighborhood crime, the loss of affordable housing units, the school's poor academic performance, dwindling programs, and competition from new charters had resulted in ongoing enrollment declines, and there were about 400 students in a building designed for 800.[12] When the school closed, students were directed to a school more than a mile away, across several dangerous intersections. Rather than navigate these difficulties, many ended up in charter schools, further eroding the funding base of the public school system. In September 2007, two charter expansion campuses opened in the building: Maya Angelou, enrolling 100 students, and Ideal Academy, with 150.[13] These two schools' total enrollment is just over half of the enrollment at Fletcher Johnson when it was declared to be "underutilizing" the space.

Another problem is that only a few of the charter schools in D.C. are community-based. These include the African-centered Roots

Academy; Next Step, begun by the Latin American Youth Center to serve high school-age mothers (see the sixth chapter in this book), and Carlos Rosario, dedicated to adult education for immigrants. But such locally based schools serving specific community needs are the exception. The majority of charter schools—and all the charter schools seeking to expand on an economy of scale—are corporate-backed entities relying on an entrepreneurial business model. Education management organizations (EMOs) and charter management organizations (CMOs) that have a foothold in D.C. include Mosaica, Edison, and the Edison-subsidiary LearnNow, all based in New York; Ohio's White Hat Management; Virginia's Imagine/Chancellor Beacon; and Massachusetts-based K12.[14]

In 2007, the California firm New Schools Venture Fund announced portfolio-level investments in 16 CMOs, including five that have targeted D.C.: KIPP-DC, Friendship Charter, DC Prep, Lighthouse Academies, and LearnNow. Another investment firm, Venture Philanthropy Partners, based in Virginia and heavily funded by the founders of AOL, also underwrites several D.C. charters: Friendship, SEED, Maya Angelou/See Forever, and César Chavez. All of these schools aspire to an economy of scale to create what KIPP has termed "city-states."[15] Although the expansionist aspirations of these charter brands are not part of the public record, CMOs reveal long-range goals in their newsletters and job announcements. In 2006, Venture Philanthropy Partners noted Friendship Charter Schools planned to open "three to four new schools in the next three to four years at a cost of $50 million and increase student enrollment by 2,000."[16] The director of DC Prep sent out a help-wanted email in 2005 noting, "over the next 10 years, DC Prep will create a model school district in the D.C. area, opening at least 10 elementary and middle school campuses, serving 2,500 students."[17]

While there is no cap on charter expansion, Congress and the City Council made eliminating 3 million square feet of public school space by fall 2008 a condition for receiving money to modernize facilities. The superintendent closed six schools in 2006 and in late 2007, the new chancellor—without community input or even meetings with the City Council—announced the planned closing of 24 additional district schools at the end of the year and the possible outsourcing of more than 20 schools to private management organizations.

Recognizing that charter proliferation was complicating reform efforts within the district's public schools, the Board of Education, which was one of two chartering organizations, twice implemented a voluntary moratorium on new charters. Clifford Janey, then superintendent, called for a citywide moratorium in 2006 but the city's other chartering organization, the D.C. Public Charter School Board, resisted. What's more, Congress's School Reform Act prohibits local officials from passing local laws designed to limit charter growth.

A look at the D.C. Public Charter School Board highlights whose interests it serves. Congress created the board, with the mayor appointing members from a list of nominees created by the U.S. Department of Education. As of 2008, three of its seven members were not D.C. residents. The board chairman, Tom Nida, lives in Virginia and is the vice president of United Bank, which has provided property acquisition and leasehold improvement loans, tax-exempt financing, lines of credit, and other services to not only the board but six charter schools and the Charter School Development Corporation, another board on which Nida sits.[18]

Problems in Charter School Quality

The unhappy result of charter proliferation has been a disconnect between the reality of charter schools performance and their reputation in the mainstream media. A look at the highly regarded School for Evolution in Educational Development (SEED) is a case in point. Founded in 1997 as the nation's first publicly subsidized boarding school, SEED now enrolls around 320 students in grades 7–12. As a residential facility, SEED receives more than $25,000 per student in tax dollars, along with sizable private donations. They have also gotten tax-exempt revenue bonds (a funding stream unavailable to the public school system but widely used by charters) and special land deals. The Prince of Wales visited SEED in 2005, and it has been featured on Oprah Winfrey, who is also one of the school's patrons. The positive publicity often focuses on their 100 percent college acceptance rates, but a close look at the numbers tells a different story.

Although SEED sends its graduates to college, it has a significant rate of expulsions and suspensions, and its practice of often retaining students at the lower grades results in a high rate of voluntary withdrawals. The school maintains an entering class of at least 40 students, but has never graduated more than 21 in a year. In 2007, only 12 students graduated.[19]

Overall, charters have done no better than the district's schools on standardized tests. In 2005-06, 118 of 146 district schools (80 percent) failed to make Adequate Yearly Progress under No Child Left Behind. Yet 30 of 34 (88 percent) charters failed. What's more, AYP mandates did not apply to 12 of the 43 schools chartered by the D.C. Public Charter School Board in 2006-07 because the school either did not serve the grades tested or their enrollment was too small to constitute a testing subgroup.[20] KIPP-DC, meanwhile, failed to make AYP at its two new campuses in 2006-07. Its flagship school, KIPP-KEY, continued to post high test scores, but KIPP also does what the district schools cannot do: retain children in lower grades based on their standardized test scores. The school's website is quite clear that even if students' overall grades are good, they may be held back if their standardized test scores don't measure up.[21]

Decline within the traditional public schools has been exacerbated by the charters' cherry-picking and dumping of students. Complicated enrollment processes allow some charters to filter out undesirable families; others engage in vigorous recruitment from existing neighborhood schools. One charter even sent letters throughout a neighborhood promising $100 to parents enrolling their child in the school.[22] Most troubling is what has become known as the "October Surprise" in local school advocacy circles: the practice of some charters of dumping unwelcome students back into the traditional public schools after the D.C. government performs an enrollment audit and "equalizes" funding. After the head count, schools keep their money, even if they later expel students or encourage their departure. Because traditional public schools must accept in-boundary students throughout the year, the district absorbs students who are pushed out of the charters. Per-pupil funding follows the students out of the public system, but fails to follow them back in.

The Problem of Equity

Money has been a particular source of tension between traditional and charter schools.

Unlike in most states, charter schools in D.C. receive not only per-pupil funding but also a per-pupil allotment for facilities. For some charters, the facilities allotment is a clear blessing because they do not have to use that money for capital expenses; they are free to use it for programs, salaries, or whatever their boards want. In addition, certain costs are shifted onto the district. Annual cost overruns in special education transportation and unfunded teacher pay raises, for instance, come out of the district budget; charter schools are unaffected.[23] What's more, beginning in 2004 Congress allocated $13 million dollars annually to each "education sector" in D.C.—charters, vouchers, and the public school system. Uniformity trumped equity, since the district's schools continue to serve the majority of the city's public school students.

Beyond budgetary concerns, there is the issue of equitable access to programs. Charter schools in D.C. do not have neighborhood boundaries, and while some have become de facto neighborhood schools, none are required to give priority to neighborhood children: attending a charter school is a choice, not a right. Navigating the list of charter schools is daunting, and many schools such as KIPP and Hyde Leadership Academy require parents to sign contracts and have a home visit before a child can be enrolled.

Lack of Transparency and Accountability

Every charter school in D.C. is a private nonprofit corporation operating with public funds, but accountable only to its own self-appointed board of trustees. The executive director of the D.C. Association of Chartered Public Schools has even declared that "charter schools are not government bodies" and are therefore exempt from Freedom of Information Act requests, open meetings laws, and so forth. Indeed, in the summer of 2006, the D.C. City Council exempted charter schools from the city's open meetings law.[24]

The meetings of the D.C. Public Charter School Board, meanwhile, are poorly publicized and rarely allow for public comment. In 2005-06 the board held one public hearing. Charter advocates claim they are more accountable to the public, but in reality, many of the schools are controlled by corporate interests and their nonprofit foundations. Joseph E. Robert Jr. provides an example of these interconnections.

Robert is chair and CEO of a real estate development company and the founder of the nonprofit education advocacy group Fight for Children. He is on the board of the Real Estate Roundtable, which lobbies Congress on behalf of real estate developers, and on the Federal City Council, which represents regional corporate interests and has been a longtime supporter of D.C. charters. He is also a principal investor in Venture Philanthropy Partners, whose efforts to expand charters on an economy of scale were described above. Other foundations with an interest in D.C. charters include the Kimsey Foundation, the Pisces Foundation, and the Walton Family Foundation, which are funded by AOL, the Gap, and Wal-Mart.[25] These groups operate outside of public scrutiny, and the extent of their involvement in the "evolution" of public education remains relatively unexplored by the mainstream media.

The Fox in the Henhouse

Charter schools are inherently shaped by local politics, and D.C. provides a good example of how interlocking corporate and gentrification agendas shape the charter movement.

In 2006 Adrian Fenty was elected mayor in a landslide, and many public school advocates hoped he would reverse the "starving the beast" policies of the previous administration. Even before his inauguration, however, the mayor met with the Federal City Council to plan a schools takeover and identify personnel. His new hires were equally problematic. They included Deputy Mayor for Education Victor Reinoso, a Federal City Council employee who won a seat on the Board of Education, and Deputy Mayor for Economic Development Neil Albert, who had been CEO of Ed Build, a private education services and construction firm, and of the New Schools Venture Fund, a key investor in the local and national charter movement.

Once in charge of the school district, Mayor Fenty selected Michelle Rhee as school chancellor, without community input and without even notifying elected officials ahead of time. An outsider who fits into the evolutionary endgame, she had only three years' experience as a teacher. For a decade she headed the nonprofit New Teacher Project, which appealed to antiunion and pro-privatization forces by advocating a simplistic approach of firing "ineffective" teachers. In early 2008, the D.C. City Council granted Rhee approval to fire nonunionized employees of the district's central office without cause. In a meeting with the Federal City Council, with whom Rhee has a close relationship, she explained, "The corporate world will be our model."[26]

The Rhee-Fenty approach is following the usual steps toward privatization: attacking public sector workers, establishing a rationale for dismantling the public school system, and claiming that the targeted public entity is bloated. But the old organizational structure has been replaced with a heavier and fatter one, closely tied to the private sector. D.C. now has two offices running the school system: the Deputy Mayor's office of a dozen senior staff members earning over $1 million a year in total salaries, and Rhee's senior staff, consisting of two senior aides with salaries totaling $200,000 and one staffer paid $75,000 a year. Rhee's annual salary was set at $275,000 with a $41,250 signing bonus and a $27,500 performance bonus. Despite all the "experts" in this extensive bureaucracy, Rhee reported that once she closes some 20-plus schools, her next step will be to consider hiring charter management organizations to run another 23 of the city's underperforming schools.

Establishing a bloated bureaucracy to run a diminishing traditional school system does not make sense unless seen in the context of the unannounced next step in the "evolutionary" scheme—Fenty and Rhee handing over all public schools to CMOs. The *Washington Post* reported on Dec. 6, 2007, that Rhee was guest of honor at a dinner party hosted by Gates Foundation executive and E. L. Haynes Charter School board member Jim Shelton. Other guests included Fenty, the CEO of E. L. Haynes, the chair of the D.C. Public Charter School Board, and Senator Mary Landrieu of Louisiana. A guest told the *Post* that the event "felt like a rallying of the troops before the war."[27]

The winter 2008 issue of *Education Next*, published by the conservative Hoover Institution, outlined the scope of this "war" on public education:

> Here, in short, is one roadmap for chartering's way forward: First, commit to drastically increasing the charter market share in a few select communities until it is the dominant system and the district is reduced to a secondary provider. The target should be 75 percent. Second, choose the target communities wisely. Each should begin with a solid charter base (at least 5 percent market share), a policy environment that will enable growth (fair funding, nondistrict authorizers, and no legislated caps), and a favorable political environment (friendly elected officials and editorial boards, a positive experience with charters to date, and unorganized opposition). ... The solution isn't an improved traditional district; it's an entirely different delivery system. ... Charter advocates should strive to have every urban public school be a charter.[28]

This article went on to identify Washington, D.C., where charters already account for 27 percent of public school enrollment, as a "potentially fertile district" where such a takeover could be implemented.

Our Save Our Schools coalition, an all-volunteer group of grassroots activists with no budget, foresaw this endgame two years ago—not because we have magical insight but because we understood that the privatization of schools was integral to the business community's goal of gentrifying D.C. It is also the logical endgame of the privatization philosophy, whether in D.C., Ohio, or New Orleans. This is why we compare these privatization schemes to global structural adjustment programs: no matter where the World Bank sends their economists, no matter what volume of data they bring back, in the end the same steps are taken toward a market-based solution: the purposeful neglect of public entities, the siphoning of public resources, the attack on public sector workers, and the false promise that a market solution is less bureaucratic, less costly, and more effective.

Unlike biological evolution, the "evolution" of public education is not inevitable. Our hope is to explain the predictable endgame of privatization plans and use that to organize a proactive grassroots defense of our public resources—focused not just on schools but affordable housing and the preservation of the public sector in general. Only this approach will clarify what city leaders have in store for us, and make it self-evident where grassroots alliances should be built.

ZEIN EL-AMINE IS A LONGPTIME D.C. COMMUNITY ACTIVIST, WRITER, AND POET. HE IS FOUNDING MEMBER OF THE SAVE OUR SCHOOLS COALITION, A GRASSROOTS ORGANIZATION COMPOSED OF TEACHERS, PARENTS, TRADE UNIONISTS, AND COMMUNITY ACTIVISTS, ENGAGED IN ORGANIZING AGAINST THE PRIVATIZATION OF THE TRADITIONAL PUBLIC SCHOOL SYSTEM IN D.C. ZEIN IS ALSO A MEMBER OF THE ELLA JO INTENTIONAL COMMUNITY COOPERATIVE—A HOUSING COOPERATIVE FOR D.C. ORGANIZERS. HE IS ALSO A FOUNDING MEMBER AND A REGULAR CONTRIBUTOR TO *LEFT TURN MAGAZINE*, A TRADE MAGAZINE FOR ACTIVISTS.

LEE GLAZER IS THE PARENT OF THREE CHILDREN IN D.C. PUBLIC SCHOOLS AND THE CO-FOUNDER OF SAVE OUR SCHOOLS. HER ARTICLES ON CHARTER PROLIFERATION HAVE APPEARED IN *LEFT TURN MAGAZINE*, *EDUCATION ORGANIZING*, AND LOCAL NEWSPAPERS, AND CAN BE FOUND AT THE SAVE OUR SCHOOLS WEBSITE, www.saveourschoolsdc.org.

Endnotes

1. Ariana Quiñones-Miranda, speaking at a Town Hall Meeting regarding the Bruce School Disposition, Advisory Neighborhood Commission 1A Monthly Meeting, Harriet Tubman Elementary School, Washington, D.C., January 10, 2006.
2. See Mead, S., "Capital Campaign: Early Returns on District of Columbia Charters," Public Policy Institute White Paper, October 2005, pp. 7–14, retrieved from www.ppionline.org/documents/DC_Charter_1004.pdf on January 13, 2008. This study was funded by a grant from the Gates Foundation; the director of the Public Policy Institute, Will Marshall, sits on the D.C. Public Charter School Board.
3. National School Boards Association, "District of Columbia Voters Strongly Oppose Vouchers, NSBA/Zogby Poll Shows," Alexandria, Va., December 10, 2002, retrieved from www.nsba.org/site/doc.asp?CID=429&DID=8579 on December 30, 2007, and "The Issues," *Black Commentator* 29, February 13, 2003, retrieved from www.blackcommentator.com/29/29_issues.html on January 4, 2008.

4. Charter legislation is ranked by the Center for Education Reform with information retrieved from www.edreform.com/index.cfm?fuseAction=state Stats&pSectionID=15&cSectionID=44 on January 4, 2008; full text of the D.C. School Reform Act can be found on the Friends of Choice in Urban Schools (FOCUS), retrieved from www.focusdccharter.org/archiveslaws/ schoolReformAct.asp on December 28, 2007.

5. National Center for Children in Poverty, "Low-Income Children in the United States: National and State Trend Data, 1995–2005," U.S. Census Bureau, 2005.

6. See D.C. Housing Authority, "Arthur Capper/Carrollsburg," retrieved from www.dchousing.org/hope6/arthur_capper_hope6.html on January 14, 2008; and Fletcher, M., "Residents Fight to Save Low Income Housing," *Washington Peace Letter* 38 (November 2001), retrieved from www.washingtonpeacecenter.org/articles/hopesixhousing.html on January 4, 2008.

7. Parents United for the D.C. Public Schools, "D.C. Public Schools Funding: Myth and Reality," and "Leaving Children Behind: The Underfunding of D.C. Public Schools Building Repair and Capital Budget Needs;" and "Civic Leaders Advisory Report, 2003," retrieved from www.washlaw.org/pdf/Leaving_Children_Behind_Report.pdf on January 29, 2008.

8. 2006 Annual Report of the D.C. Public Charter School Board, retrieved from www.dcpubliccharter.com/publications/docs/PCSB_AR2006.pdf on December 27, 2007, and FOCUS, *D.C. Public Charter School Bulletin*, October 30, 2006, retrieved from www.focus-dccharter.org/archiveslaws/ archivesNewsletters.asp on January 12, 2008.

9. JCAHO, the hospital accreditation board, gave D.C. General a rating of 94 out of 100 in 2000, higher than Georgetown University Hospital or Washington Hospital Center. See "Report of Health Care Now Coalition," March 2001, retrieved from www.dcwatch.com/issues/pbc0103c.htm on January 29, 2008.

10. See Dingerson, L., "Unlovely," p. 17.

11. FOCUS, *D.C. Public Charter School News Bulletin*, November 2, 2007, retrieved from www.focusdccharter.org/archiveslaws/archivesNewsletters.asp on January 4, 2008.

12. The 21st Century School Fund, *Better Buildings*, June-July 2006, retrieved from www.21csf.org/csf-home/publications/emails/BetterBuildingsJune-July2006.pdf and www.21csf.org/csf%2Dhome/datashop.asp on January 29, 2008.

13. FOCUS, *Charter School Directory*, retrieved from www.focusdc.org/charter schooldirectory/directory.asp on January 4, 2008.

14. This top-down approach has been a hallmark of the national charter movement as well. See Wells, A.S., Introduction to *Where Charter School Policy Fails: The Problems of Accountability and Equity*, (New York: Columbia University Press, 2002) p. 11.

15. Robelan, E.W., "KIPP Schools Shift Strategy for 'Scaling Up'," *Education Week*, April 12, 2006.

16. Venture Philanthropy Partners, "Friendship Public Charter School: Investment Summary," retrieved from www.vppartners.org/portfolio/friend ship/summary.html on January 12, 2008.

17. "Come Grow with Us," forwarded email from Emily Lawson, Director of DC Prep, July 16, 2005.

18. See, e.g., "FOCUS Vendor Fair for Charter Schools," February 7, 2007, retrieved from www.focus-dccharter.org/documents/vendor_fair.pdf on January 13, 2008.

19. D.C. Public Charter School Board, "2006 Annual Report" and "2007 Annual Report," retrieved from www.dcpubliccharter.com/publications/annualrep.html on December 27, 2007; Hopkinson, N., "SEED's Harvest," *Washington Post*, June 29, 2004, p. C-1, retrieved from www.washington post.com/wp-dyn/ articles/A16283-2004Jun29.html; SEED Foundation, "About the SEED Foundation," retrieved from www.seedfoundation.com/about_seed/history.aspx; Sinzinger, K., "Is SEED School Worth the Money?" *Common Denominator*, May 1, 2006, p. 1.

20. D.C. Public Charter School Board, "2006 Annual Report" and "2007 Annual Report," p. 19, and D.C. Public Charter School Board School Performance Reports for 2005–07, retrieved from www.dcpubliccharter.com/publications/spr.html on December 27, 2008.

21. See KIPP-Key Academy Parent-Student Handbook 2005–06, retrieved from www.kippdc.org/files/docs/ParentStudentHandbook06-07.pdf on January 29, 2008.

22. "A Special Gift for you of $100.00" flyer, Barbara Jordan Public Charter School, August 7, 2006. Available from: www.saveourschoolsdc.org.

23. See Nelson, F. H., et al. "Paying for the Vision: Charter School Revenue and Expenditures," National Charter School Finance Study, American Federation of Teachers Educational Foundation, May 2003, pp. 105–114.

24. Pitts, E., "Time for D.C. to Catch Up," *Common Denominator*, June 12, 2006, p. 1. See also Stewart, N., "Vote on New Open-Meetings Law Looms," *Washington Post*, June 7, 2006, p. B-2, retrieved from www.washingtonpost. com/wpdyn/content/article/2006/07/06/AR2006070601609.html on January 26, 2008.

25. See Sen, B., "Corporate Puppeteers: A Look at Who's Behind the Charter School Movement," *Left Turn Magazine*, October/November 2006, pp. 50–54.

26. See Jaffe, H., "Can Michelle Rhee Save D.C. Schools?" *Washingtonian*, September 1, 2007, retrieved from www.washingtonian.com/articles/people/5222.html on January 12, 2008. Thanks to Gina Arlotto for calling this article to our attention.

27. Stewart, N. and Nakamura, D., "Educational Gathering," *Washington Post*, December. 6, 2007, p. DZ-1, retrieved from at www.washingtonpost.com/wp-dyn/content/article/2007/12/05/AR2007120501010_pf.html on January 13, 2008.

28. Smarick, A., "Wave of the Future: Why Charter Schools Should Replace Failing Urban Schools," *Education Next*, 8 (Winter 2008), retrieved from www.hoover.org/publications/ednext/11130241.html. Thanks to Leigh Dingerson for sharing this article.

Boston's Pilot Schools:

An Alternative to Charter Schools

DAN FRENCH

At Another Course to College, a Boston Pilot high school, a focus group of students recently was asked by a team of visitors, "Why did you come to this school?" The eight students, racially diverse, responded with similar themes. "Teachers are always available to help me out." "The teachers are demanding, we read college texts, but they give you the individual attention you need." "My teachers know me, they expect great things of me, and I want to do well to show them they are right."[1]

Put aside, if you want, the reports and figures which demonstrate the overall success of the Boston Pilot Schools initiative. Listen to the students and you will understand what other schools and urban districts can learn from Boston's Pilot Schools.

The Pilot Schools were created in 1995 through a partnership of the mayor, the superintendent, the Boston Public Schools (BPS) school committee, and the Boston Teachers Union. Spurred in part by Massachusetts' legislation enabling charter schools and the potential loss of Boston students, the BPS called on the Pilot Schools "to provide models of educational excellence that help to foster widespread educational reform in all Boston public schools."[2]

For 11 years the nonprofit organization which I direct, the Boston-based Center for Collaborative Education, has coordinated this voluntary network of Pilot Schools on behalf of the school district and teacher union. Why have we chosen this unique role?

Under the federal legislation No Child Left Behind, most urban public school districts have increased centralization through mandated instructional practices, required textbooks, and frequent testing. Yet centralization, coupled with the time-bound roles of school districts and teacher unions in mandating policies and setting uniform work conditions, has most often continued a pattern of low achievement, particularly for low-income, black, and Latino students. At a time when families across race and income have become more disenchanted with urban public school districts, many districts are experiencing rapid enrollment decline due to a rise in charter schools. I believe the Pilot Schools model has the potential to be a powerful model of reform in urban districts.

What Are Pilot Schools?

Pilot Schools are a direct outgrowth of the charter movement, yet provide an alternative to the privatization efforts of many charter management organizations. Different than charters, Pilot Schools are located within existing school districts and teacher unions. At the same time, the Pilot model requires school districts and teacher unions to give up historical control and grant schools and those who work in them the power to make their own decisions to best meet students' and families' needs. The model is essentially one of teacher and parent empowerment.

By virtue of an innovative "thin contract" provision, Pilot Schools have charter-like autonomy over budget, staffing, governance, curriculum, assessment, and the school calendar, and are exempt from district policies and mandates. Teachers who work in Pilot Schools are exempt from teacher union contract work rules, while still receiving union salary, benefits, and accrual of seniority within the district.

Pilot Schools receive a lump sum per pupil and can choose discretionary services from the central district or have the equivalent per-pupil amount added to their budgets. They can hire inside and outside the district without regard to seniority, and create their own staffing patterns and job descriptions. Pilot Schools set the school schedule and calendar for both students and faculty. While the schools are held to state tests, the curriculum and assessments they use to prepare students are up to them.

Pilot governing boards include the administrator and faculty, parent, student, and community representation. They are akin to a nonprofit board of directors—they approve an annual work agreement for faculty, set the school vision, approve the annual budget, and hire and evaluate the principal (with the superintendent retaining final authority).

Beginning with four Pilot Schools enrolling 600 students in 1995, there are now 20 schools, preK-12, that enroll more than 6,700 students, or 12 percent of the district enrollment. These 20 schools represent an early childhood center, three preK-5 or K-5 elementary schools, four K-8 elementary schools, two middle schools, one 6-12 secondary school, and nine high schools. Pilot transportation is the same as for all BPS students—buses for elementary and middle school students, and bus and subway for high school students.

Almost every school is small, enrolling 450 students or less, enabling greater personalization. As one Pilot student stated, "Here, I can go to somebody when I need someone to talk to and know that person is actually concerned and that person is going to help me."[3]

All Pilot elementary and middle schools enroll students through the district lottery system, while the 10 Pilot high schools use a variety of enrollment processes. Two have a lottery similar to other nonexam Boston public schools (Boston has three public high schools with strict admission procedures), two have referrals and target students who have previously been academically unsuccessful or who have dropped out of school, one is a 6-12 school and five have "academically blind" applications designed to ensure a match between the school's mission and the student's interest (i.e., Students submit an application, but schools are not allowed to select students based on prior academic achievement. One school, a performing arts high school, holds auditions as well.) Contrary to popular belief, application Pilot high schools serve a slightly higher percentage of entering 9th graders with high risk factors than do lottery Pilot high schools.[4]

Many Pilot Schools are entrepreneurial, successfully raising "soft" money to support their programs, although they represent a spectrum in their fundraising efforts. Several Pilots have even established their own 501(c)(3) nonprofits in order to strengthen their fundraising efforts. On the whole, Pilot Schools probably raise more external funds than do regular district schools, because of their entrepreneurial spirit and their appeal to outside funders. However, there is a range; there are successful Pilot Schools which raise fewer external funds, as well as those that bring in substantial additional revenue.

Teachers in Pilot Schools

Teachers voluntarily choose to work at Pilot Schools; they annually sign an "election-to-work agreement" which stipulates the work conditions. Because Pilots are exempt from conditions in the union contract, every Pilot School is required to have a process on how teachers may resolve a dispute with the administration. Normally, the process includes meeting with the principal and teacher union school representative (elected by peers), followed by meeting with a subcommittee of the governing board. The final step lies with the superintendent and teacher union president; in 12 years, only one dispute has reached this level.

In the early years, many Pilots struggled to develop clear election-to-work agreements. As a result, a networkwide teacher committee worked with the Center for Collaborative Education to develop a template agreement that Pilot Schools could individualize. More recently, a contract amendment guaranteed a minimum of four teachers on every school's governing board.

Because many charter schools experience significant teacher turnover, some worried this would also occur with Pilots, given the longer hours and multiple roles given to staff. The union also raised concerns that the Pilot practice of budgeting actual salaries would result in hiring younger teachers and releasing more veteran teachers as they rise above the district's average salary. To address these concerns, the BPS Budget Office annually tracks the average salary of each Pilot School. It has found that Pilots experience a similar trend as regular schools—startup schools tend to hire a starting staff that is less experienced than mature schools, and as years pass they trend upward toward the district average salary.

Certainly, in a network of 20 schools, there are outliers. A few Pilots have had significant leadership issues and, much like any regular school in the same situation, have experienced high faculty turnover. Compared to charters, however, Pilot Schools are more likely to have a more stable faculty, according to Susan Moore Johnson, a Harvard University education researcher. She posits that this is because the Pilot work load requirements are usually less than those of charters and Pilot faculty have more protections, including salary, benefits, seniority, and an election-to-work agreement.[5]

Pilot Schools: Making Their Mark

In November 2007, the Center for Collaborative Education released a four-year, student-level study on the performance of Pilot students as compared to students in regular, nonexam Boston public high schools, *Strong Results, High Demand: A Four-Year Study of Boston's Pilot High Schools*.[6] The study found that Pilot students outperformed the district average in the nonexam high schools on every student engagement and performance indicator measured, and across race, income, and academic subgroups, including entering freshmen with risk factors. Due to their higher attendance (94 percent to 89 percent), Pilot students attend school an average of two weeks longer than their regular school peers. Pilot students' four-year graduation rate for 2006 was more than 23 percentage points higher than their traditional BPS high school peers, 75.7 percent as compared to 52.2 percent.

On the state's high stakes standardized test, Pilot students outpace their regular school peers in both English and math, at every grade level tested. On the 2006 state English test, Pilot 10th graders' passing rate was 23 percentage points higher than that of regular 10th graders, 83 percent to 60 percent.

Particularly important is the fact that the performance in Pilot high schools of students with high risk factors (low attendance, over-age, and/or failure of the 8th-grade state math test) significantly outpaces that of their peers in regular district high schools. For example, in math, Pilot 10th graders who had failed the state's 8th-grade math test passed the 10th-grade math test at almost 20 percentage points higher than their regular high school counterparts (70 percent to 51 percent).[7]

The study found that Pilot enrollment generally matches that of the district by race, income, and mainstream special education. Pilots lag behind the district in enrolling moderate to severe special education students (4 percent in Pilots versus 10 percent in regular public schools as of 2005), English Language Learners (3 percent versus 16 percent), and students with risk factors in the 8th-grade. However, almost half of all entering Pilot freshmen failed the state's 8th-grade math test (48 percent in Pilots versus 59 percent in regular schools) and Pilot numbers of moderate to severe special needs students are beginning to rise due to a recent district and Pilot initiative to ensure equitable enrollment.[8] While it is not possible to isolate how much the difference in performance between Pilot and regular high schools stems from Pilot conditions and characteristics as opposed to differences in population, clearly Pilot Schools are making a difference if students in every subgroup tested—by race, income, and students with risk factors—are doing better in Pilot Schools.

The study also examined the effect of application versus lottery on enrollment patterns in Pilot high schools. While in their first year Pilot lottery high schools enrolled a higher percentage of 9th graders with 8th-grade risk factors, by the third year these percentages were below the average for application Pilot high schools. One reason was found in choice patterns. The two Pilot lottery high schools had two of the highest rates of applicants versus available seats in the district (7.3 applicants per seat for Another Course to College and 4.1 for TechBoston Academy). Furthermore, at a time of declining enrollment in the district (a trend common to many urban districts across the nation), 25 percent of entering Pilot freshmen were not enrolled in the Boston Public Schools the prior year (many coming from charter, private, and parochial schools.[9] The study concludes that "students and families [across race and income] who are searching for a college preparatory education disproportionately select high-performing high schools."[10]

Why the Promising Findings?

Why are Pilots experiencing compelling results across race, income, and risk factors? I believe it is because Pilot Schools can place their resources where they feel it matters most. In most Pilots, premium value is placed on (1) personalizing learning in the core academic classes, and (2) establishing a strong professional collaborative culture focused on improving instruction. As a result, Pilot Schools have:

- Low student-teacher loads (55-60 students per teacher) and class sizes (18 in Pilot 9th-grade English versus 28 in regular high schools) in core academic courses.
- Longer amounts of instructional time (392 minutes per day versus 380 in regular high schools).
- Substantial time for staff collaboration (an average of 285 minutes per week in Pilots versus 29 in regular high schools, and six professional development days in Pilots versus three in regular high schools).
- Substantial wraparound student support—advisors, learning centers, and student support teams.
- Graduation through mastery, including exhibitions, portfolio reviews, internships, research projects, and demonstrations.[11]

With limited resources, there is a trade-off for these decisions. In most Pilot Schools, electives and course offerings are spare. Teachers and administrators assume multiple roles, with fewer specialists. Inter-scholastic athletic offerings are few. Yet the core academic benefits are unmistakable and for most students far outweigh the drawbacks.

Many have asked which Pilot autonomies are most important. Our answer is all of them; they are interdependent. Staffing autonomy is critical to hiring a staff that is unified around a common vision. Yet this autonomy means little if you don't have the budget flexibility to reallocate staffing patterns to match the vision. Similarly, curriculum flexibility is critical to designing a culturally relevant college preparatory curriculum, but this means little if you don't have the scheduling flexibility to create the professional development time to teach it effectively.

In the early years, Pilots were kept on the fringe of district activity. In more recent years, with the sustained success that Pilots have experienced, the district has looked for ways to learn from the Pilot experience. The Pilot concept of small size was used to divide four large comprehensive high schools into multiple small (non-Pilot) high schools. And several forums for sharing among Pilots and regular schools have been held. However, the inroads in sharing among types of schools have been spare, and much progress in this area needs to be made.

Advocacy and the Role of the Network

The road to launching Pilot Schools was difficult, and there was little if any district realignment to support the initiative. Every proposed change became a negotiation between individual schools and central office—budgets, facilities, curriculum, transcripts, and more. Central office administrators treated Pilot Schools as regular schools and resisted new course titles, narrative report cards, and inclusion practices, just to name a few of many examples. Too often, Pilot principals felt stymied in implementing the autonomies they thought they had won.

In the spring of 1997, the Center for Collaborative Education hosted a weekend retreat for Pilot leaders, who realized they needed to unite if they were going to carve out the full scope of autonomies. Thus was born the Boston Pilot Schools Network, with the center adopting a coordinating role. The Pilot Schools informed the district that going forward they would speak with one voice. This newfound unity enabled the Pilot Schools to codify needed autonomy.

A new model was created of a nonprofit coordinating a subset of schools within an urban public school district. The relationship between the center and the Pilot Schools is voluntary. While the center holds no authority over the Pilots, several Pilot principals serve on the center's Board of Directors. After several years, the network set up an annual fee for the center's services. However, this fee generates only about 10 percent of the roughly $1.3 million annually the center devotes to the Pilots; all remaining funds are raised by the center from foundations.[12]

The center serves the Pilots by providing onsite coaching, professional development, district negotiations, financial management, community advocacy, and research. It has advocated on the behalf of Pilot Schools to negotiate a lump-sum, per-pupil formula for each grade span, with access to central discretionary funds (about $2-3 million networkwide per year); leverage substantial external grant funds (about $10 million over 10 years); set flexible human resource policies; create a school quality review process of accountability; and gain freedom from numerous district policies.

Practitioners learn best from other practitioners, school leaders and teachers alike. The center facilitates opportunities for teachers and principals to share practices and problem solve through monthly leadership meetings, an annual two-day spring leadership retreat, and opportunities for teachers to share instructional practices.

Obstacles Along the Way

Despite the Pilot successes, along the way we have encountered our share of obstacles and frustrations. Here are several:

Time-bound district culture. The Pilot School initiative reflects the natural tensions between a group of innovative schools and the larger district of which they are members. The district often perceives the Pilots' lack of conformity as arrogance, while the Pilots believe the district's attempts to make them conform are impeding true reform. While the superintendent supported the Pilot model, there has been little management unity below this position. Many freedoms would not have been attained without the center and the Pilot network that banded together at the negotiating table. Encroachment efforts to curb specific autonomies are common after 12 years, and there is still considerable central management resentment that Pilots operate by a different set of rules.

Hybrid, district-mandated Pilot Schools. Pilot Schools are intended to be voluntary, shaped by teams of faculty, administrators, parents, and community members. Yet in 2003 the school district decided to give Pilot status to two newly constructed neighborhood schools. While there was a design team selection process, the district mandated many elements of each school—size (750 students), rollout at full enroll-ment, disproportionately high placement of English language learners and moderate to severe special needs students as compared to the dis-trict averages, and rollout during a year of double-digit budget cuts, resulting in hiring in August for a September startup, with 30 percent of faculty involuntarily assigned due to layoffs and bumping rights. Needless to say, both schools have struggled mightily to overcome these obstacles.

Weak governing boards. Governing boards have been one of the most uneven components of the Pilot model. While some Pilots have strong governing boards, with clear decision-making roles and ample repre-sentation from community groups, other Pilot boards have struggled. Some have been ill-equipped to take on principal hiring and annual evaluation, others to engage in long-term strategic planning, still others to facilitate the annual process of revising and approving the election-to-work agreement for faculty. In recent years, as a result, the center has organized much more significant training for governing boards. Overall, the need remains high for more attention to creating Pilot governing boards with strong, diverse representation, clear roles, and a visionary direction.

Lack of a defined intervention process. When any movement grows beyond a few schools, schools with low student achievement, weak leadership, and/or high faculty turnover inevitably occur. To date, the center has been unsuccessful in partnering with the district and teacher union to co-develop an intervention process that would result in supportive yet directive assistance to struggling Pilots.

Lessons Learned

Regardless of one's overall view of charter schools, one clear benefit lies in the external pressure they have placed upon some school districts and teacher unions to search for innovative ways to improve schools; this is especially important given that too many districts have resisted change.[13] In working with Boston's Pilot Schools, the Center for Collaborative Education has learned the following valuable lessons, which we take with us as we begin to replicate the model in other districts such as Los Angeles.

Lesson One: *School districts and teacher unions need radically new partnerships that result in fundamentally different schools.* Public schools as we know them today are on the decline. Boston, similar to many other urban districts, has lost over 10 percent of its enrollment in seven years. During this time, the percentage of school-age Boston youth who are enrolled in charter, private, parochial, or suburban schools has increased from 20 percent to 27 percent. Yet Pilot Schools' enrollment continues to grow. Boston's parents and students are voting with their feet for a different breed of schools—small, safe, personalized, academically challenging, and democratic. If school districts and teacher union do not change to meet this trend, they may be left behind.

As Tom Mooney, recently deceased president of the Ohio Federation of Teachers, said in an interview: "What [teacher unions] have to do now is … realize that it's not good enough to be limiting the power of the bureaucracy; we have to transform it … or we'll be out of work. Public schools won't survive, at least in urban areas, unless we really make some radical changes. We [teacher unions] have to be in the forefront of making those changes."[14]

The Pilot Schools model has the potential to be a centerpiece of this transformation. As one Pilot principal stated, "What every [school] should have are the kinds of conditions Pilots have. That's everything from size and scale to hiring their own staff to instructional flexibility to governance, the works."[15]

Lesson Two: *Incrementalism does not lead to fully autonomous schools.* The Pilot Schools illustrate the power of giving a school a complete set of tools to undertake comprehensive reform. As other school districts explore replicating the Pilot concept, it is common to look for ways to engage by stages. However, seeking a schedule change, or a side letter union agreement for revising a job description, or a waiver request from a textbook requirement, will not lead to the full scope of autonomies, nor will such incrementalism allow staff to consider how teaching and learning can be different. In districts that have tried an incremental approach, the process has bogged down at the first stage, never to progress.[16]

Lesson Three: *Pilot Schools should be founded upon the principle of equity.* Charter schools have often faced criticism that certain groups of students have less access to enrollment—students with moderate to severe special needs and English language learners, for example. It is incumbent upon Pilot Schools to demonstrate that independent-minded schools can serve the democratic mission of serving all students who arrive at their doors. Pilot School enrollment should reflect that of the larger school district, across race, income, language, and special education status. In Boston, the tension of lottery versus application at the high school level is best resolved through instituting a districtwide student assignment process that maximizes the match of all students with all schools, such as 8th-grade high school orientation sessions or courses for every student.

Lesson Four: *The community needs to be a partner at the table in order to keep the district and teacher union focused on access and equity for all students.* Although the community was not part of the original partnership that spawned the Pilot Schools, community groups have played an important role in sustaining the Pilots. Key community groups have rallied around the model and called on the district and teacher union to create more, while helping to fend off attempts of encroaching upon Pilot autonomies.

Lesson Five: *Accountability goes hand in hand with autonomy.* Given the tenet that schoolwork should have real-life application, Pilot students are assessed through multiple measures, including portfolios, exhibitions, performances, and comprehensive research projects with the goal of building students' capacity to perform real-world tasks. In this way, Pilot Schools strive to use their assessment measures to prepare students for future work and civic engagement.

To measure school progress, Pilot Schools have instituted a five-year cycle of school quality reviews that tracks effective practice and student outcomes. During the cycle, each school conducts a self-study assessment based on a set of benchmarks, resulting in a school portfolio reflecting the school's progress. An external team of practitioners then conducts a three-day onsite visit, and submits a report of findings and recommendations to the school district and teacher union.[17]

Lesson Six: *Networks of like-minded schools can play a powerful role in creating successful schools.* Over the years, the Pilot Schools have collaborated to influence one another's practice through monthly leadership meetings, spring retreats, annual teacher sharing conferences, study groups, and cross-school visits. As one Pilot School director said: "It's a whole different conversation. ... We're reading articles, we've talked about solving educational problems. We're talking about policy. We're talking about critical friendship. We're talking about the issues that we really should be contending with.[18]

Lesson Seven: *Third-party intermediaries can provide valuable assistance to a network of autonomous schools.* Intermediary organizations can play a vital role in building alliances among like-minded schools, and help them to navigate district bureaucracies while creating opportunities for sharing. Serving as a "jack-of-all-trades," the Center for Collaborative Education supports the Pilot Schools through coaching, professional development, advocacy, research, and even financial management, while facilitating district negotiations on budget, policy, and resource allocation.

Lesson Eight: *Scaling up the numbers of Pilot Schools challenges the very partners who created them.* For both the district and teacher union, Pilot Schools were easier to support when they were few in number. The district was able to implement its centralized, one-model approach to school reform, while keeping the Pilot Schools comfortably on the margins.

With growth and success come challenges. Within the district, budget, curriculum, and governance autonomy threaten central office managers. Deputy superintendents lack supervisory control over Pilot principals (unless requested by a governing board); the district cannot mandate curriculum to Pilots; and many central departments resent that Pilot Schools may choose additional funds rather than purchasing their services. In the absence of an understanding of the Pilot model, growth becomes threatening.

Within the union, officials fear that Pilot expansion will call into question the larger contract conditions. If teachers can staff schools in which work conditions are defined at the school rather than district level, and these schools are demonstrating compelling outcomes, what are the implications for the larger district contract?

Considering the Future

The Pilot Schools model is centered upon creating personalized, equitable, and autonomous schools that are unified in their service of children and families. Ultimately, its growth calls into question the existence of school districts and teacher unions as we presently know them, challenging these institutions to recast themselves. Central offices would be reconfigured to be service-friendly to schools, rather than monitor-oriented. In addition to negotiating districtwide salaries and benefits, teacher unions would assist faculty to build professional collaborative cultures with supportive work agreements, rather than negotiating a uniform set of work conditions for every school.

Influenced by the charter school concept, the Pilot model may have the necessary traits and promising outcomes to gain much-needed traction within traditional public school districts, where the vast majority of our students still go to school.

DAN FRENCH IS THE EXECUTIVE DIRECTOR OF THE CENTER FOR COLLABORATIVE EDUCATION, A NONPROFIT ORGANIZATION DEDICATED TO CREATING PERSONALIZED, EQUITABLE, AND AUTONOMOUS PUBLIC SCHOOLS SERVING HIGH PERCENTAGES OF LOW-INCOME STUDENTS AND STUDENTS OF COLOR. HE WAS FORMERLY THE DIRECTOR OF INSTRUCTION AND CURRICULUM FOR THE MASSACHUSETTS DEPARTMENT OF EDUCATION. HE HAS WRITTEN NUMEROUS ARTICLES, INCLUDING THE LEAD STORY IN THE NOVEMBER 1998 PHI DELTA KAPPAN, "THE STATE'S ROLE IN SHAPING A PROGRESSIVE VISION OF PUBLIC EDUCATION."

Endnotes

1. November 2005 focus group with Another Course to College (ACC) high school students. ACC is a Boston Pilot school.
2. Boston Public Schools memorandum on Pilot Schools, fall 1995.
3. BCLA student focus group, May 2005.
4. Tung, R. and Ouimette, M., *Strong Results, High Demand: A Four-Year Study of Boston's Pilot High Schools.* (Boston: Center for Collaborative Education, 2007).
5. Johnson, S. M. and Landman, J., "'Sometimes Bureaucracy Has Its Charms': The Working Conditions of Teachers in Deregulated School," *Teachers College Record*, 2000, 102(1): 85-124.
6. Tung, R. and Ouimette, M., 2007. The data reported on were received from the Boston Public Schools and Massachusetts Department of Education, and the report's findings were reviewed by an external advisory group of prominent education researchers.
7. ibid.
8. ibid.
9. ibid.
10. ibid.
11. Tung, R. M., Ouimette, M., and Rugen, L., *Progress and Promise: A Report on the Boston Pilot Schools* (Boston: Center for Collaborative Education, 2006).
12. CCE has never received any district funds to support our Pilot coordination. CCE has, though, received BPS contract funds to work with other BPS schools, including its small, non-Pilot high schools.
13. Buddin, R. and Zimmer, R. W., *Charter School Performance in Urban Districts: Are They Closing the Achievement Gap?* (Santa Monica, CA: RAND Corporation, 2005).
14. Interview by Claudia Levin with Tom Mooney. *Primer*, KnowledgeWorks Foundation, January 2007, vol. 2, no. 1.
15. As quoted in Parson, G. and Brown, N., "Chapter IV: The Pilot Schools," *The Boston Annenberg Challenge: Baseline Evaluation Report* (Cambridge: Education Matters, Inc., 1999).
16. French, D., "Progress and Promise in Urban School Reform: Boston's Pilot Schools," *Education Week*, May 2006.
17. French, D., *The Boston Pilot Schools Self-Study Guide for Use with the School Quality Review Process* (Boston: Center for Collaborative Education, 2005).
18. As quoted in Parson, G. and Brown, N., 1999.

Lessons from the Ground:

Interviews with Charter School Educators

BARBARA MINER

The following is condensed from interviews with educators from three community-based charter schools. Those interviewed are:

Debbie Wei, *principal of The Folk Arts—Cultural Treasures Charter School (FACTS) in Philadelphia.* FACTS opened in September 2005, chartered by Asian Americans United in association with the Philadelphia Folklore Project, two long-established community organizations. The goal was a multiracial K-8 school serving the specific needs of immigrant populations, fostering an appreciation of learning, culture, and community, and implementing an art-based, culturally sensitive curriculum. Website: www.factsweb.org.

Rob van Nood, *teacher, 3rd-4th-5th Intermediate Grades, Trillium Charter School in Portland, Ore.* Trillium was founded in 2002 by parents and teachers with educational philosophies rooted in the democratic school/freeschool movement. A K-12 school with a tuition-based preschool, Trillium describes itself as a "democratically structured environment that fosters students' natural curiosity, creativity, and self-awareness. Students learn to take initiative and assume responsibility for their own learning, which supports constructive interaction with the local, regional, and global community."
Website: www.trilliumcharterschool.org.

Linda Ohmans, *former principal of The Next Step/El Proximo Paso in Washington, D.C.* The Next Step was started by the Latin American Youth Center, a 26-year-old educational and social service organization. Opening in 1998, the school serves students ages 14-21, with a special focus on teen parents and young people who have dropped out of other schools. It believes that young people learn best in small schools, with a curriculum relevant to their lives and a staff sensitive to the student's culture and the obstacles students face as they try to stay in school. Ohmans was the school's principal from its founding until November 2006. Website: www.layc-dc.org/charterschools/nextstep.html.

Why did you opt for a charter over a traditional public school? Were there specific union or district regulations you wanted to avoid?

Wei, *FACTS in Philadelphia:* It took us a long time to decide because we had all these concerns about how charters were being used by the right and by privatization interests. But we had been so frustrated with education reform within the district. You would go through these protracted struggles, finally get what you want, and then the superintendent would change, or the principal would change, and everything you fought for would be deep-sixed. We couldn't attain lasting, sustained change in any place that we organized.

Another problem was the inability of schools to choose teachers. The Philly union contract was a straight-up seniority system and it didn't matter if you created this particular vision, because you were basically beholden to the seniority system and whoever felt like coming in could come in.

A third factor was the district's failure to meet the needs of immigrant kids and their families. We won a lawsuit against the district, basically around inequitable access to education for non-English speaking students, and that suit was filed in 1985. Twenty years later, they are still working in committee to address the issues raised. We were not suing for money but equitable services. But that was when I was young and naive. Now I realize that when you ask for equitable services in an underfunded district that doesn't work for poor students, immigrants and nonimmigrant alike, asking for equity goes only so far.

Van Nood, *Trillium in Portland:* The founding people were part of what was called the Sunnyside Cooperative School. It was a public elementary and middle school, but it was located in another elementary school's building and the principal of that school had a very different philosophy of education. There was constant tension and a lot of families left. A group of teachers and several parents with children in the school felt that given the tensions, the school would not be able to maintain a progressive vision. So they decided to try a charter.

In terms of district and union rules, the main issue had to do with being able to hire staff who fit with our philosophy. Before we were charter, you had people on staff who were either not understanding the school's philosophy or didn't care. They had moved into the position because there was an opening. The district allowed the school to develop its own philosophy, but if you don't have the right staff, that doesn't work.

Personally, I am pro-union and that was one of the hardest things for me to accept coming to the charter school. I gave up the union so I could teach the way I want to teach.

Ohmans, *The Next Step in Washington, D.C.*: At the time we applied to be a charter school, I was the director of the teen parent program at the Latin American Youth Center. The program was a combination of social service support for teen mothers and an educational program geared toward young parents either learning English and hopefully going back to a regular school, or passing the GED. It had been working really well for five years, and the director of the Youth center pushed the idea of converting to a charter school. We didn't even know what that meant, it was all so new. But it seemed that what we were doing in the teen parent program was alternative education and that was an ideal of charter schools at the time. It didn't have anything to do with union and district regulations.

We also had the idea, and I think people still have the idea, that it would be great if there were a way that the school could be a model for other public schools in the district. One of the reasons we are able to keep the kids in the school is that we provide a variety of social services supports, and that could be a model. We work closely with other neighborhood agencies, health clinics; we help students find daycare; we provide stipends so the girls can pay their own babysitters at home; we have two social workers—and we had five years of experience in knowing the extra support that teen mothers need.

What have you gained by operating independently of the public school system?

Wei, *FACTS in Philadelphia*:   One of the things we gained was the power to come out from under the district's mandated curriculum. Philly's public schools were taken over by the state and are run by this School Reform Commission. Philly doesn't have a superintendent, but we have a CEO and a business model, with a mandated core curriculum tied to test preparation. As a charter, we can not only hire our own teachers but also implement our curriculum according to our mission and our respect for language and culture and social justice. As it stands in the district right now, we would not have been able to do that.

Van Nood, *Trillium in Portland*: Problems with the district's curricular approach is a big part of why I came to Trillium. Within the Portland district, there has been a strong standardized testing push in the last 10 years, coupled with mandated programs. One friend in the Portland public schools told me that under the district's mandates, there are tight restrictions on what you can use to teach reading because of their contract with an international textbook publisher. Say you are doing a reading unit that involves bread; this person was afraid to even bring in someone who is a baker, or show a video, unless it came from the textbook publisher. At Trillium, in contrast, we can build a curriculum based on individual students' needs and interests.

Most important, however, is that we have been able to build a school run by the people involved in it every day—the students, staff, and parents.

Ohmans, *The Next Step in Washington, D.C.*: Control of the curriculum is one of the most important issues for us, as well. We place a strong focus on using the experiences and stories of our students to shape the curriculum. We use their life stories to teach writing, U.S. history, reading comprehension, and English as a Second Language, as well as to inspire other areas of study and provide the connections that the students need to stay in school. Portfolio assessments have become an anchor for our school and are increasingly driving our instruction. To help keep students in school, we have a work experience program that includes workshops on how to get and keep a job, job shadowing, and paid internships. We believe so strongly in this connection between the curriculum and the real world that we have a full-time staff person dedicated to the program.

Our curriculum is constantly in motion because so are our students. The curricular freedoms come with challenges, but the freedom also inspires creativity.

What are your student demographics?

Wei, *FACTS in Philadelphia*: The school had about 400 students in 2007-08 in K-7, with plans to expand to K-8 next year. All our students are accepted through a straight-up lottery. Sixty percent of the students are Asian (Chinese, Indonesian, Vietnamese, Cambodian, Lao), 35 percent are African-American, and about 5 percent are Latino immigrants, although some are African immigrants from Liberia. And there are a handful of white students. Overall, 92 percent of our students qualify for free or reduced lunch. About 30 percent of the students are English language learners, with all teachers trained to provide ELL support; about 10 percent of the students require special education services, although the special ed figures are hard to know for sure because there are students we think may require special services, but have not yet been formally identified.

Van Nood, *Trillium in Portland*: We admit students through a lottery, unless they have a sibling already at the school, and then they get first priority. We also ask that parents and the students spend a day at the school before they come, just so they understand the school's philosophy. About 35-40 percent of our students are low-income and qualify for the federal lunch program, about 16-20 percent are special ed, and less than 1 percent are English language learners. Overall, about 75 percent of our students are white and 25 percent students of color. In the 2007-08 year we have about 320 students in K-12, with an additional 40 in the preschool.

Ohmans, *The Next Step in Washington, D.C.*: About 85 percent of our students are Latino, primarily from Central America, and 15 percent are African-American. Occasionally, there have been Asian students. In the 2007-08 school year, about 13 percent of the students receive special education services, 80 percent are English language learners, and 99 percent receive free or reduced lunch. The school has about 84 students. We're one of the smallest of the charter schools in D.C., but we think our current enrollment is about right for what we want to do.

What are your relations with the broader community?

Wei, *FACTS in Philadelphia*: When we decided to do a charter, we specifically chose to locate it in Philadelphia's Chinatown. One of the reasons was the lack of publicly funded institutions in the community. There is no traditional public school in Chinatown, no health center, no recreation center. We have 4,000 residents and about a quarter are youth and there are no such facilities. On top of that there is gentrification that is pushing out families. So we wanted a strong public institution in our community.

A few years back, Asian Americans United worked with others to defeat a proposal for a baseball stadium in Chinatown. In fact, our school is located in the footprint of that proposed stadium.

It is hard for folks to do things in the community when they don't control the properties, but in this case we had a community businessman who owned the space, was concerned about gentrification, and wanted to build a community institution. He got a lot of offers to turn his space into condos or hotels. When we approached him he said he would hold the building for us if we could get the charter. He took on the risk and helped with the renovation of the building. He said, "If this is the only way we will get an institution in the community, I will do it." It's a nice story because it highlights certain things about our school and its centeredness in the community. Because of gentrification, we would not have been able to afford a place for the school if Mr. Wong had not stepped forward.

Van Nood, *Trillium in Portland*:   Our school is open to anyone in Portland, and our community is centered on our educational philosophy. We also have a community representative on our board. Within the school, we have a strong emphasis on democratic decision-making and student and staff say in the school. The staff, led by the director, makes most of the decisions about the school program; for instance we decide what classes will be taught, who will teach them, the schedule, and so forth. Staff meetings are run collectively, with rotating responsibilities, and most decisions are made as a group. The staff and students created the school constitution, which is modeled after the U.S. Constitution and puts a lot of power in the hands of staff and students.

Ohmans, *The Next Step in Washington, D.C.*: We are affiliated with the Latin American Youth Center, which was founded in the late 1960s, and our school is located in their building. In addition, one of our board members is from the Youth Center, and a couple of others are community representatives. Our relationship to the Youth Center and to the community make us very different from charters that are part of a national franchise.

Our connection to the Youth Center also allows us to tap into their programs, so under the same roof we have a number of wraparound services such as a counseling program and after-school activities.

What about staffing issues such as certification and teacher turnover?

Wei, *FACTS in Philadelphia*: Our teachers are not part of the union, although by law they have comparable healthcare benefits. By law, up to 25 percent of the charter school teachers do not have to be certified but in our school, 95 percent are certified. We are actually like the haven for progressive teachers who can't take it anymore in the Philadelphia district.

Van Nood, *Trillium in Portland*: When we became a charter, flexibility in certification was a big issue, partly because we wanted to bring in staff that were experienced in different areas, especially community-based people, but who might not be certified. While certification fluctuates from year to year, about 75 percent of our staff are certified and have a master's degree.

We are not part of the union, and, as with other charters, pay and benefits are decided by the school. The founders of Trillium want a good pay scale, and for newer and midlevel teachers the pay and benefits are comparable to what Portland offers. We haven't been able to have as high a ceiling for top pay, however.

Staff turnover was somewhat of an issue the first several years. We were a startup charter and, on both sides, people wanted to make sure there was a good fit. In recent years, turnover has not been an issue. I know a lot of charters have had problems with so many beginning teachers, without enough veterans to provide support and help keep things stable. We've been lucky because we have about half and half, in terms of younger versus experienced teachers.

Ohmans, *The Next Step in Washington, D.C.*: Most of the teachers are certified, most have masters', and all but two are bilingual. Math and science have always been the hardest positions to fill. In terms of staff turnover, it has been very, very low. There are lots of reasons, but one is that we want our salaries to be competitive with the public schools; we pay about $1,000 a year less, partly because our school is so small that we have little budget flexibility. Hopefully, our teaching environment and the voice the teachers have in the operation of the school make up for that. We also raise our pay scale when the public teachers get a raise.

How has the federal No Child Left Behind (NCLB) act affected your school?

Wei, *FACTS in Philadelphia*: The mandated testing is a big issue. We do certain types of test preparation, because kids can't walk into a test and do well if they have never seen standardized tests before. NCLB has also cost us money in the sense that there is communication required to go home and we are not reimbursed for any of the costs—in particular because we routinely translate documents into four languages: Chinese, Indonesian, Vietnamese, and Spanish. And then there's the issue of how Adequate Yearly Progress is determined. We have not met AYP in any given year, partly because we're so new and a lot of our students are playing catch-up. Last year we didn't make AYP because of our African-American subgroup, so we are looking hard at achievement gap issues. Also, the state keeps changing what you need to meet AYP.

Ohmans, *The Next Step in Washington, D.C.*: For our students, NCLB hasn't had a huge impact. You need a certain number of students to have a testing subgroup, and we rarely have enough, partly because we have such a wide range of ages and, for different reasons, our population is very transient, and also because we're a small school. So we've been able to keep a focus on shaping our curriculum around our students' needs.

How do you relate to the public school system or other charters? How are the lessons you have learned transmitted to other schools?

Wei, *FACTS in Philadelphia*: Overall in Pennsylvania, the conservatives and Republicans pushed charter schools. The schools themselves tend to be a mixed bag—in terms of the number of charter schools as a group in Philadelphia, we constitute the second largest district in the state. There are a number of charters that, quality-wise, are not very good. And there are a number that are very good. All of the charters tend to be safer than the Philadelphia public schools. In terms of philosophy, there are schools that speak to the cultural or political needs of the students and communities they serve, but there are also the Edison and KIPP type schools.

I have informal contact with some of the more progressive charters, and there are a few I email a lot.

One principal I communicate with a lot called me this weekend. They have an Indonesian student whose family is slated for deportation. She knew we had a lot of experience working around immigrant rights and picked my brains about how to do organizing work on behalf of the family. There's a lot of that kind of informal support that I have with a few schools.

There has been some talk of trying to coordinate professional development among the charters, but that hasn't happened. People are so overwhelmed trying to keep their schools going. We pay fees for this charter school coalition in the state, but their politics are a lot more conservative than ours. Actually, a lot of the charter schools are more conservative than we are. So, it's great to have a coalition for some things, but we aren't all necessarily kindred spirits.

Van Nood, *Trillium in Portland*: One of the directives of the charter school law in Oregon is that charter schools will attempt to bring what they have learned to other schools. But we haven't had much direct contact with other public schools because it's hard to find avenues for that. We moved into a new location this year and in the old location, we tried to have a relationship with the middle school there but it didn't really go anywhere for a lot of reasons. For one, the principal was open to a conversation, but wasn't overly excited about making it happen. And it was a struggling middle school, which is now being reconstituted as an all-girls high school. So it already had its own struggles and there wasn't the time to build a partnership.

There aren't any formal structures, so everything has to be done by the schools themselves. Trillium got a federal dissemination grant and we hosted several conferences to talk about what we are doing. But for the most part, the people who come are from charter schools, whether in Portland or other districts.

At this point, there's not a lot of interaction with the Portland public schools. My sense is that some in the professional teaching community see us as a kind of thorn in the sides of the schools, and think we are stealing their kids away, stealing their resources, and so forth. They don't greet us with open arms. There is more of an interest from families, especially when they feel their kids aren't making it and need other options.

As far as charters, we are a bit in a bubble in Portland, so I feel I can talk positively about charter schools. In Portland, we don't have a lot of the Edisons or other commercially oriented charters. Portland charters are pretty progressive philosophically, and not into scripted, back-to-basic curriculums.

Overall, we are trying to prevent Edison-type schools from coming into the state. We don't feel we have much in common with the conservative, privatization charters and don't want them to gain a foothold in the state.

Ohmans, *The Next Step in Washington, D.C.*: Our contact with other schools is minimal. There has never been any mechanism to share what we are doing, either with traditional public schools or charter schools. We had cordial relations with other charters, but we didn't share much in common. Our situation was somewhat unique. When we started we had this beautiful space to move into in the Latin American Youth Center building—everything was there, from the security, to the accounting, to the janitorial services. Other charters, meanwhile, were looking around for decent space, sometimes temporarily housed in a church basement or something like that. For most new charters, finding space is an incredibly consuming problem. In addition, we work with high school students, the only charter to do so in that beginning stage. Finally, our students are primarily Latino although admission is open to any student who applies on a first-come, first-served basis. That's not true of a lot of the charters.

While we never saw ourselves as promoting a model to be replicated, at the same time when we realize something works we often find ourselves saying, 'Gee, there's no reason this couldn't be done elsewhere.' There's no reason, for instance, why a high school of 3,000 students couldn't be divided up into schools of 1,000 each. Or no reason not to have more social counselors and other support services, which are absolutely critical for young parents. Or no reason not to have a strong bilingual program where students can be taught core academic classes in Spanish at the same time they are learning English as a second language.

A strong point of our school—and there's no reason why it couldn't happen in other schools—is that there is a sense of ownership among the staff. Everyone feels responsible for how the school turns out.

BARBARA MINER HAS MORE THAN 30 YEARS' EXPERIENCE AS A WRITER, COLUMNIST, AND EDITOR FOR NEWSPAPERS, MAGAZINES, AND BOOKS. A FORMER MANAGING EDITOR AND CONTINUING COLUMNIST FOR RETHINKING SCHOOLS MAGAZINE, SHE WRITES OFTEN ON EDUCATION AND OTHER SOCIAL ISSUES. HER WRITINGS HAVE APPEARED IN PUBLICATIONS FROM THE NEW YORK TIMES TO THE NATION, THE PROGRESSIVE, COLORLINES, MILWAUKEE MAGAZINE, AND THE MILWAUKEE JOURNAL SENTINEL.

Keeping the Promise:
The Role of Policy in Reform

LINDA DARLING-HAMMOND AND KENNETH MONTGOMERY

> Charter school reform enjoys support from constituents not typically found in the same political circles. ... Though these stakeholders support the reform, they approach it based upon what are often vastly different social and political values.
> —Janelle T. Scott and Margaret E. Barber[1]

Ted Sizer and George Wood opened this book by reminding us of the four fundamental values that underlie our system of public education: equity, access, public purpose, and public ownership. These four values are critical to the demands of a democracy for an educated citizenry, and they provide a means to evaluate reforms such as those promised by the charter school movement.

One of the central concepts of charters is the value of individual choice in spurring student and parent commitment to their schools, as well as broader system reform. Yet choice raises knotty and profound issues. What happens when choice initiatives create schools that are not worth choosing—and may even harm some students? Or when schools of choice will not "choose" students who are not sufficiently high-achieving, well-supported at home, or otherwise viewed as a "fit" for the school? What are the implications when public schools are allowed to exclude? Or exacerbate segregation? Can we design schools of choice that serve the broad purposes of public education?

In this chapter, we examine the role that policy can play in answering such questions. Although charters are often discussed in monolithic terms, the policy frameworks that create them vary substantially, and these policy choices are related to the wide range of outcomes emerging from charter schools and other forms of school choice.

Philosophical Foundations

The charter movement occupies a relatively unique place among education reforms. It embodies two distinct and at times contradictory theories of action. To some, charter schools are primarily a method for creating an educational marketplace. To others, charter schools are primarily a way to free educators from overly burdensome bureaucratic constraints while maintaining the context of democratically accountable institutions. The philosophical differences are visible in state policies, some of which favor a market ideology while others place more emphasis on democratic values and the importance of a strong public sector.

The marketplace approach assumes that the market is best equipped to reform public education. Presumably, individual schools will be motivated to provide a better product so that they will not lose customers (students), and education as a whole will improve as schools compete against one another to create more attractive products. An underlying assumption is that public education will deteriorate if not guided by the market, because students and families will not have the freedom, as consumers, to choose from a variety of possibilities.

In this view, charter schools also give stakeholders the chance to exit schools they do not like. The threat of exit is expected to put competitive pressure on the traditional system to improve or risk losing students.[2]

The principles of the free market also look to increase parental involvement, not necessarily within the organization of the school, but as consumers forcing the school to respond to their needs. At root is a belief that quality is primarily grounded in the competition of the marketplace.

The free-market philosophy treats public education largely as a private commodity rather than a public good; individual schools meanwhile are seen as businesses whose major concern is getting and keeping customers. The philosophy does not address the question of what happens to students if their schools fail in the Darwinian marketplace. Nor does it focus on broader purposes of schooling: preparing students to participate effectively in the political, social, and economic life of the nation, including how we form a public that can talk, work, and make decisions together.

By contrast, Sizer and Wood describe a democratic theory of action for choice, which attends to the principles that individuals should have the power to shape their public institutions by voicing their preferences and holding their leaders accountable through direct democratic processes. This theory of action is based on the idea that charter schools (or other public schools of choice, like the Boston Pilot Schools) can improve education by supporting innovation and freeing educators and parents from unnecessary bureaucratic restrictions. It suggests that innovative practices in schools of choice can help create new forms of education that inform the larger public school system. Proponents of this view contend that the major problem is not the lack of incentives for effort, but the pressures for standardization that stifle new approaches.

They also feel that democratic mechanisms play an important role in overseeing schools to ensure equitable access and outcomes. Parents are not viewed primarily as consumers, but are expected to be involved in their children's education. The hope is that schools of choice will increase educational quality and equity not by increasing the exit option, but by reducing bureaucratically imposed constraints and by giving parents a greater voice in school improvement. When conceptualized in this manner, the primary objective of schools of choice is to enable educators and parents to work together more closely, while protecting students' rights of access and guarantees of basic educational quality.

It is a delicate balancing act to give charter schools the freedom to innovate and hold them accountable without recreating unnecessary bureaucracy. There also are inherent tensions in fostering competition based on individual choice without compromising the public purposes of education. These purposes require schools to help develop a citizenry that can live together productively, embracing the values that undergird our pluralistic democracy. The record of charter schools reflects such complexities.

The Track Record of Charter Schools

According to the National Alliance for Public Charter Schools, in the 2006-07 school year 40 states and the District of Columbia had a combined 4,046 charter schools serving 1.1 million students across the nation. Four hundred charter schools opened in that year, representing a 12 percent increase from the previous year. The chapters in this volume include examples of both successful and unsuccessful charter schools as judged against criteria ranging from student access and provision of high-quality learning experiences to outcomes such as student achievement and graduation. These mixed results characterize most of the research on charters. As Scott Imberman of the University of Maryland found in his review of evidence on achievement and student behavior outcomes in charter schools:

> [S]ome researchers find insignificant or negative impacts of attending a charter school (Hanushek, Kain, Rivkin and

Branch, 2007; Bifulco and Ladd, 2006; Sass, 2006; Zimmerand Buddin, 2003), while others find positive impacts (Booker, Gilpatric, Gronberg and Jansen, 2007; Hoxby and Rockoff, 2004; Solmon and Goldschmidt, 2004; Solmon, Paark and Garcia, 2001). Thus, we might conclude from these studies that the effect of charter schools on academic performance is, at best, unclear.[3]

Other reviews of research report similar findings,[4] noting the differences in outcomes across different states, which suggests the potential effects of varying policies.

Most analyses of charter schools have treated them as a monolithic group, rather than evaluating the features of the individual schools in the context of the state policies that shape equity, access, responsiveness to public purposes, and public ownership. Within the context of these core values, we examine the charter policies of Arizona, Louisiana, Ohio, and the District of Columbia as examples of a market-based philosophy. We look at the policies of California and Minnesota as examples of a more democratically rooted philosophy, and those of Wisconsin—where Milwaukee is subject to different rules than the rest of the state—as a mixed case. In doing so, we surface some of the inherent tensions between policies that aim primarily to foster competition and those that are more focused on the pursuit of public engagement and innovation.

It is also important to underscore that policies are not always neatly categorized as fostering competition or democratic principles. How charters develop in a particular state or district is related to larger political forces. State policies may work toward equity with one policy, but undermine the effort with other policies. There are many factors in creating equitable systems.

Public Ownership

We begin with the concept of public ownership. The ways in which policies shape this aspect of school governance predict many other school features and outcomes. Sizer and Wood emphasize the integral relationship between public ownership and local control: "public schools were to be governed closest to the people they served, requiring little need to trek to the state or federal capital for redress of grievances."

It is not just that schools are "public" in the legal sense of the term (they receive public funds, are nonreligious, and do not charge tuition). Another essential concept is that public schools must function in a way that allows students, families, and the general public easy access to those with authority over the school. This philosophy of public ownership contains an implied accountability mechanism. If the school is not serving the people, the people can easily voice their concerns to those in power.

Perhaps nowhere else is the tension between using competition to foster innovation and the need for some degree of regulation more apparent than through the lens of public ownership. One of the main ways that state policies approach this issue is through the number and variety of charter authorizers.

Authorization and charter contracts. The essence of all charter school law is a contract between a founding group and an authorizer. Some states allow multiple authorizers, while others give local districts the power to develop charter schools. States also vary in the extent to which they require participation and endorsement from local parents or teachers in the creation of charters.

Ohio allows for more types of organizations to become authorizers than any other state. There are currently more than 65 authorizers in the state, and over 50 percent of charter schools in Ohio have been sponsored by nonprofit entities not connected with any public agency. As result there has been an "explosive proliferation" of charters, leading to concerns about both quality and accountability.

While some states require extensive parent and community participation in establishing the charter, others require little or none.[5] For example, Arizona, Massachusetts, Michigan, Nevada, Oklahoma, Oregon, and Ohio require no parent or teacher input either for start-ups or for converting a traditional school to a charter.

In practice, a wide-open authorization system appears to foster a more competitive environment, as states with multiple authorizers have an average of eight times as many charter schools as do states with a single authorizer.[6] However, this approach may also create unintended consequences, as suggested by abuses that have surfaced in Ohio, where some schools have been created that provide little service to students or exclude those they do not want to serve.

To develop effective accountability, state policies must ensure meaningful contracts between the charter school and the authorizer. A democratic theory assumes that local charter authorization makes it easier for the community to monitor charters not just during the approval process but also during the school's operation. In theory, local monitoring should increase accountability and school quality because stakeholders will be able to communicate more easily with those running the school (and will have a local entity to go to if they are unhappy with the way the school is functioning); they will be able to better gain information, and school leaders in turn will better understand how to serve their constituents.

Of course, this works in practice only when the stakeholders have sufficient information and power to be heard and when school leaders have sufficient incentives to be responsive. Key considerations in this regard are whether the school is required to work with an authorizer who knows and has a stake in the community, and whether constituents have easy access to the chartering authority.

California has built a significant charter sector by relying largely on local school district boards as authorizers.[7] Prospective schools must present signatures from interested local parents and teachers. Local school boards must review educational and financial plans before granting a charter. California allows the state board to approve charters that have been denied by the local board and the county board, but those decisions are subject to judicial review,[8] which creates a fairly high level of scrutiny. Although California policy also allows charters exemptions from many state rules, the local chartering board must monitor budgets, teacher qualifications, and achievement, and verify that a number of state and federal laws are met. The local superintendent sits on the board of each charter authorized in his or her district.

Minnesota allows a wider array of authorizers, which includes local school boards, public and private colleges, and district cooperatives. However, nonlocal authorizers such as postsecondary schools must have third-party consent. Minnesota also requires that teachers form a majority on the board that receives the charter. Finally, Minnesota allows charter schools to maintain their contract for a maximum of three years, while California requires renewals every five years. By contrast, charters are granted for 15 years in Arizona and Washington, D.C.[9] Shorter contracts may enhance public ownership by allowing the public to weigh in regularly on a school's performance.

In the mixed case of Wisconsin, sole chartering authority rests with local school boards, with the exception of Milwaukee (the state's largest school district), where a wider range of authorizers is permitted. Unless the school is a board-initiated charter, no school can be authorized without approval from 50 percent of the teachers in a school or 10 percent in a school district. Local districts are held accountable for their chartering decisions. The state does not grant charters, nor does it hear appeals for denied applications. This has historically helped keep chartering processes close to local communities, with most of the early charters initiated by parents. However, the distinctive rules for Milwaukee have recently encouraged more outside providers, including for-profit owners, to enter the state, so the landscape appears to be changing.

By conceptualizing chartering largely as a local grassroots activity, California, Minnesota, and Wisconsin have built a number of charter schools that are responsive to parents and teachers. Some may argue that this has come at the expense of even more competition, but policy makers in these states have tended to value public ownership as much as competition.

The importance of effective monitoring. Effective monitoring requires a clear, easily accessible line of communication between charter authorizers and constituents. When local monitoring is difficult, charter authorities tend to rely on fiscal management and standardized tests as their primary means of accountability. Responsible fiscal management is important, but it can be easily obscured, as Amy Hanauer illustrates in the Ohio case (see p. 35). A 2007 report from researchers at Arizona State University, meanwhile, found it is often difficult to get financial information from for-profit private charter management companies because of their desire to keep their operations secret from competitors.[10] Multisite management companies also tend to aggregate data from all their schools into a single report,[11] and sometimes argue that they are not subject to state public records or public audit laws.

Despite its efforts to create public ownership through local authorization, California has had difficulty with fiscal monitoring. In 2006, the California Department of Education began an attempt to recover $57 million from a chain of independent study charter schools that for three years overcharged the state. The chain had authorizations from eight local districts, but was still able to overcharge.[12] While local boards may have some advantages in monitoring local charters, they operate with limited resources. State policies may need to take the difficulties of monitoring into account and provide stronger guidelines for reporting and more resources for monitoring.

At the same time, fiscal management does not provide insight into the core functions of the school: teaching and learning. Evaluating whether students are receiving a quality education (or whether harder-to-educate students are being counseled out) is even more difficult. As Sizer and Wood point out, standardized testing accountability mechanisms can be problematic for assessing the diverse educational programs offered by charters. Aside from the many issues associated with the limited content of most tests, there are limitations with the ways in which data are aggregated and made publicly available. For example, the use of average test scores to evaluate charters can mask differences and changes in student populations, and may create incentives to keep out or counsel out low-performing students.[13]

Because of their small student bodies, unusual governance structures, or educational configurations, many charters may fall into system loopholes that exempt them from reporting requirements. For instance, studies of academic achievement of charters in the Great Lakes states have found the Ohio data difficult to analyze because of the large number of schools and students for which no data are available.[14]

While it is impossible to draw a direct relationship between the governance structures of charters and their academic outcomes, a recent study found that, overall, charter schools in Ohio were consistently performing at levels lower than their demographically similar public school counterparts, whereas charters in Minnesota and Wisconsin were performing slightly above their demographically matched peers in most areas.[15] Another study confirmed these results for Wisconsin and found lower performance at the less well-regulated charter schools in Washington, D.C. and Arizona, controlling for student socioeconomic status.[16]

A recent study in California, meanwhile, found charter outcomes varied by type, with middle and high school charters scoring above and elementary charters scoring below their demographically similar peers.[17] Equally important from a governance perspective is the fact that, after adjusting for student characteristics, classroom-based charters significantly outperformed nonclassroom-based charters—those that provide a substantial portion of their instruction through home schooling, independent study, or distance learning.

Equity and Access

For Sizer and Wood, equity involves examining the school's admission policies and the access granted to students once they enter the school. They note that, "equity may not mean 'equal,' but rather that each child should have access to the educational resources he or she needs to be successful." In addition to a school's instructional program, school funding and enrollment provisions influence how these critical values play out. By focusing on these two areas, one can see how some charter policies may foster more equitable and accessible systems than others.

Funding. There are substantial equity and access implications of governmental approaches to charter school funding, linked in particular to whether states view charter schools as a strategy for competition and cost-cutting, or, alternatively, as a means for democratic engagement that develops higher quality and greater innovation. Most data indicate that, in general, charter schools receive less funding than traditional public schools.[18] However, there is a substantial range in funding strategies. For example, charters in Minnesota are funded at a level of 102 percent of traditional public school funding, whereas charters in Ohio receive only 69 percent of average public school funding and no startup funds.[19] This discourages the development of local "mom and pop" charters and favors better-capitalized outside educational management organizations (EMOs). Indeed, two-thirds of Ohio's charter students attend EMO schools.[20] Ohio's policy uses the market to provide a less costly way for the state to educate students, whereas Minnesota policy assumes that the state has an important role in funding charters equitably to safeguard the quality of education for children.

California charters are funded at a level just under the average per-pupil expenditure in the state, although many are located in more costly urban areas. A recent study of California charter schools found that most are unable to survive strictly on public funds and that a school's ability to raise private funds was influenced by the social class of its students,[21] a finding that has implications for equity in serving students.

Admission policies and choice. If access is to be meaningful, charter policies should prevent schools from sorting and selecting students and from excluding those who are harder or more expensive to educate. Charter schools are typically given considerable autonomy in designing their programs and recruiting their student bodies, which can create inequities. If charter schools conceive of themselves as competitive, free-market entities, they are likely to engage in admission practices that decrease their costs and increase efficiency; if charters are intended to fulfill democratic goals, they will be expected to serve all students equally, and perhaps to construct better integrated student populations.

Comparing California and Minnesota with other states shows the different attitudes toward such issues. California prohibits selective enrollments and charters are allowed to give preference only to siblings and students in the charter's district. Charters are also required to design recruitment and lottery systems so that the racial balance of the charter will be reasonably similar to that of the district. Minnesota has a similar racial balance requirement.

Such policies stand in contrast to initial charter rules in Louisiana, where one-third of new charters in the spring of 2006 had selective admission policies.[22] Although push-back against the Louisiana policy has reduced the number of formally selective schools, there are still many that are tacitly selective by virtue of not being handicapped accessible or providing services to disabled students, or requiring contracts from parents and students that can prevent entry or hasten expulsion. Similarly, in Michigan, where management companies run 70 percent of charters, there is evidence companies attempt to steer clear of high-cost students, creating homogenized schools and shifting charters to the suburbs.[23]

The most responsible charter policies require that charters are open to all students in the district, with a lottery for an oversubscribed school. This prevents schools from denying admissions to students who might be more costly to educate, such as students with special needs. Lotteries are also preferential to the "first come, first served" policies used in some states because such policies privilege students with more assertive parents and easy access to better information.[24]

Recent studies have concluded that because of targeted recruitment, charter schools have more power than most public schools to shape their communities.[25] Given this, it is important that charter school policies prevent schools from ignoring some groups as they recruit. Certainly, there are delicate tensions in managing the access issue, because charter schools are often targeted, themed schools designed to serve a specific type of student. Allowing charter schools the freedom to attract communities of students who will be successful at their schools within the guidance of open admission policies appears to be a useful compromise, but challenges in implementation cannot be avoided.

Finally, even where state policies try to promote equal access to charters, certain groups have more resources than others to obtain information about schools. All choice systems inherently involve free-market principles and the assumption that consumers will be making an authentic choice. In practice, however, the market often fails in this regard. A recent study of parental choice in Milwaukee found that only 10 percent of parents exercised choice based on adequate and accurate information about schools' academic performance.[26] And, as some researchers have noted, it is particularly difficult for parents with limited English proficiency "to learn specific details about their children's schools even with the added incentive of choice. The lack of easy information may overwhelm most other factors."[27]

The challenges of choice are illustrated by a Texas study which found that the majority of Anglo students were in academically oriented charters, while most minority students were in vocational charters.[28] Students in academic schools were more likely to report that their family made the placement decision, and more than twice as many students of color (46 percent) than white students (22 percent) said they chose their own school, presumably with little parental involvement. Choice is a much different process for those who are well connected to the market than for those who have less information and access. If a state views charter schools as a way to increase competition, it must also create mechanisms to ensure true choice for the different members of society.

Another issue arises when charter policies allow for the conversion of private schools to charter schools. This can increase options, but there have been cases of private schools converting to charter schools primarily so the students' families do not have to pay tuition and without changing their admissions policies to allow full public access.[29]

Because charter schools have a special opportunity to shape their school communities, it seems fair to expect that they promote full access rather than just prohibiting admissions policies that sort and select on forbidden categories. Without a proactive approach, there is no reason to assume that access to education for traditionally underserved groups will be any better than their access in markets such as housing and labor. As Erica Frankenberg and Chungmei Lee of the Harvard Civil Rights Project write, "Without other equity provisions built into this market-based reform, charter schools are unlikely to overcome the persistent segregation of our larger society. ... One could say that the normal outcome of markets in a racially stratified society is a perpetuation of racial stratification."[30]

In addition to stable and adequate funding, the key components of an equitable choice policy include open admission with proactive information outreach and recruitment of all groups of students. Given the nation's history of discrimination, charter school policies should also be reviewed to assess their impact on students of color, even if the policy is racially neutral on its face. Finally, there is also the reality, often forgotten in the discussion of choice and charters, that many families choose the traditional public school for reasons of academic quality, location, or special features of the school program. All of the considerations we've described here should apply to these "schools of choice" as well.

Public Purpose

What is the public purpose of public education? Sizer and Wood suggest that "our schools should be places where all children gain skills for lifelong learning and engaged citizenship." At the founding of the United States, in the debates over whether a people could create and sustain democratic rule, Alexander Hamilton offered this argument for a representative rather than a popular democratic form of government: "Thy people," he told Thomas Jefferson, "are a beast." Thus challenged, Jefferson argued that "the people" could be prepared to govern responsibly through a system of public education that would develop an intelligent populace. Public schools—which would prepare citizens to debate and decide among competing ideas, to weigh the individual and the common good, and to make judgments that could sustain democratic institutions and ideals—would enable the people to make sound decisions and withstand the threat of tyranny.

Jefferson's argument and our democratic foundation rest on a kind of schooling that goes beyond "basic skills" or literacy. Schools must cultivate in all students the skills, knowledge, and understanding that give them the capacity for independent thought, for living productively together, and for embracing the values essential to a pluralistic democracy. This requires creating diverse communities of young people who learn with and about each other, as well as educating students to respect the rights of others and take up their responsibilities as citizens. There is nothing in chartering that precludes the attainment of these goals, but accomplishing them requires some thoughtful policy construction in a context that has the potential to place individual preferences or private interests above communal goals.

Meeting the demands of consumers will always be a major focus of a competitive system and, without a moral compass, can sway schools to behave in more exclusionary and less democratically purposeful ways. Without some expectations for inclusiveness and for curriculum focused on the democratic mission, chartering runs the risk of allocating public resources to parents, advocates, and school leaders who are "pushing particularistic self-interests, while neglecting the 'common good.'"[31]

Currently, in many states the only mechanism that binds charter schools to the common goals of education is the system of test-based accountability, which, as Sizer and Wood point out, does little to advance the public purposes of education. Proponents of a democratic approach have argued that charter schools should be accountable for outlining in their charters how they will fulfill public goals of inclusion and citizenship.

Some states require that charters describe how their curriculum will meet state learning goals and standards as part of the chartering process, including civic goals; how they will strive to construct a diverse student body; and how they will work with parents and community members. Many new high school models—whether charter or part of the traditional system—emphasize community service and community-based education strategies that engage students in civic life. These kinds of strategies heighten the probability that all our public schools will serve the public good.

Innovation

Given the interest in innovation that drives much of the rationale for charters, Sizer and Wood propose that it should be an explicit goal. They argue that "charters must provide genuine regulatory relief as a system to report widely on their innovations and results. Any policy that drives charters into old molds undermines the intent of charter schools." This philosophy sees charters primarily as a way to experiment with and improve educational practice. While some states, like Wisconsin, specify in their laws that innovation should be a central objective in approving charters, not all states prioritize this goal. In a market framework, innovation in some schools might be one byproduct of competition, but not a necessary component of all schools.

Innovation and entrepreneurial space. State policy makers are having difficulty managing the tension between fostering innovation and holding schools accountable to the other purposes of public education—equity, access, development of citizenship—without recreating unnecessary bureaucracy. One critical aspect of the state's role is to ascertain that students are being adequately taught to become productive citizens of society. But how can this be done without inappropriately constraining the curricular choices of schools?

It is unrealistic to assume that states can manage all of the expectations of public education without regulating charters in some ways. Indeed, a 2002 survey by the U.S. Department of Education found that "40 percent of charter schools reported not having authority over curriculum and the school calendar and 30 percent reported not having full authority over assessment and discipline policies."[32]

Among the issues that have emerged is the regulation of curriculum and assessment. Currently all states use the same standardized test measures to assess charter schools as are used in traditional public schools. Many argue that to the extent these measures drive the curriculum (which is likely when there are high stakes attached for schools or students), this decreases school innovation and autonomy. A different approach, initiated in the way alternative schools have been regulated in New York, is to permit schools not wishing to use state standardized tests to develop and implement defensible assessments of student learning, approved by the state, and to document school outcomes. The Performance Standards Consortium in New York, which grew out of the work of a group of schools administered by the New York City alternative schools division, has developed its own graduation portfolio of challenging research papers, investigations, and exhibitions. The Consortium also conducts research on student graduation and college-going outcomes, including following students for several years after high school.

Policies may need to envision new ways of documenting school practices and outcomes—and disseminating evidence about practices and their effects—if the goal of innovation is to be more than rhetorical.

Innovation and competition. Competition can provoke innovation under certain circumstances. For example, a recent newspaper article in California reports that a small, affluent school district that had rejected a parental request for creating a Mandarin language immersion program decided to go ahead with the program after the parents threatened to create a charter school.[33] At the same time, however, there is little evidence of widespread learning between the two sectors. A recent study in California found that traditional public schools feel charters have an unfair advantage because of the flexibility they are afforded, and there is little direct communication between organizations in the two sectors.[34]

Where this is true, schools in one sector—charter or traditional—may not gain from breakthroughs that occur in the other sector because they are not gaining access to them. Furthermore, where innovations *are* made possible by relief from regulations, they cannot spread unless the same regulatory relief is applied to other parts of the system. Few states have examined ways to deregulate public schools in ways that might permit greater innovation while preserving core public values. Often as charters are being created to permit flexibility in one part of the system, heavy-handed regulation is increasing apace in the other part of the system.

When charter schools are conceived primarily as competitors in educational markets, they are likely to engage in practices similar to those found in other competitive markets—and indeed, local districts in the competitive marketplace may do the same. These practices do not necessarily improve all organizations, but are designed instead to allow one organization to limit the effectiveness of another.

Because of competitive pressures that limit the sharing of information among sectors, the research community has been left with much of the onus of figuring out what can be learned from charter schools and other schools of choice. The research agenda has primarily focused on governance structures and school organization but little is known about teaching and learning in charter schools.[35]

Conclusion

The different theories of action that undergird proposals for charter schools have led to different policy strategies for creating and managing charters. It is clear that competition is an important driver behind some state charter policies, and while stimulating change, it can also have high costs and can lead to abuses. Democratic principles for chartering preserve important public purposes, but they require regulation. The most useful policies and practices find ways to foster innovation without compromising equity, access, and public purpose—developing methods for public ownership that keep charters close to the people they are meant to serve.

We believe this can be accomplished if policy makers are thoughtful about the goals of public education in a democracy and about the ways they can pursue these goals. First, it is important that public ownership be conceptualized in a way that maintains proximity to those being served and provides oversight from agencies that have both a commitment to the public goals of public education and a capacity for effective monitoring. Since charters are contracts between schools and their authorizers, authorizers must be as connected to the local community as possible. Charter applicants should work closely with authorizers to develop a contract that best serves and is accountable to the local community.

Using agencies other than local boards to authorize charters may increase competition. But it also increases distance from the local community and may lead to uncorrected abuses, such as students who are underserved but lack redress, fiscal problems that are uncorrected, or access that is manipulated to exclude those who are deemed less desirable students. Experience suggests that when the authorizers are distant from the school, monitoring becomes more costly and less effective.

Finally, permitting for-profit entities to operate public charters should be questioned; there is an inherent conflict of interest in an enterprise that, in order to maintain profit margins, must continually decide which services can be reduced or eliminated or which students will not be served because they are too expensive to educate.

If schools are to serve the public good, it is critical to demand open admissions policies and practices, and to disallow selective admissions that hold the seeds of a privatized system in which schools are separated by their ability to choose their students, rather than by the ability of students and families to choose their schools. Charters should be monitored to ensure that they do not push or counsel out students who present educational challenges.

As part of a commitment to equity, states should ensure reasonable funding to charter schools—pegged to the norms for traditional public schools, so that charter students are equitably and adequately served, and incentives are not created for fiscally nonviable operations. At the same time, resources for charters should not come at the expense of local districts that authorize them, as is the case in some places, like California, where districts must provide facilities and oversight to charters without adequate state funding to cover the costs. If all schools are to improve as a function of chartering, it is important to ensure two-way collaborative relationships that foster shared responsibility. In this regard, it is important to recognize that innovations worth spreading are not limited to charter schools.

Supporting innovative practices by balancing free-market principles and democratic accountability may seem especially difficult, but it is at the heart of the charter movement. As the Boston Pilot Schools and the New York City alternative schools have illustrated, this is not impossible. Both of these are existing proof that large public organizations can create organizational firewalls that allow space for innovation. But to do so they must always be conscious of the impact of their policies on school-level practice and they must, over time, allow innovators to help change the rules as well as to avoid them. While New York state, after much contention, now allows schools in the Performance Standards Consortium to use an intellectually powerful graduation portfolio in lieu of a set of largely multiple-choice tests, other schools cannot substantially change their curriculum practices without similar opportunities. The geological dig of policies that holds the current system in place is equally constraining to traditional public school systems and to new schools of choice—whether they are in the charter sector or not.

Ultimately, the challenge is to create a system filled with schools worth choosing and that are open to all. Many schools, local districts, and school reform networks have been tackling this challenge for years, often with significant success.[36] Such efforts do not reap profits for entrepreneurs, but they reap benefits for all, including those who may feel removed from the children and parents who are directly served. When central city high schools graduate virtually all of their students and send most of them on to college, as some of these "break the mold" schools are able to do, everyone wins: other students, whose aspirations are lifted; local communities, whose streets are filled with more determination and less despair; and people everywhere, who pay lower bills for welfare and prison cells while their Social Security receipts are secured by a greater number of young people entering the workforce as productive taxpayers rather than tax-users.

Many new charters have learned from these models of successful public schooling, just as some traditional schools have learned from practices created through the charter process. All of these efforts need the protections from bureaucratic micromanagement and political changes that are afforded to charters, just as all schools need the supports and expectations that recognize education as a public good, not a private commodity. We require all students to attend school so that they will be prepared to participate effectively in the political, social, and economic life of our country. The public welfare—not just the individual's pocketbook—is served when young people become productive, responsible citizens.

The question the public should ask as it searches to redesign our schools is, "Where's the public good?" As we discover affirmative answers in the efforts of school reformers who work on behalf of all children, we should make sure that both investments and protections follow. The real bottom line is that when all our children are well educated, the entire nation will benefit.

LINDA DARLING-HAMMOND IS THE CHARLES E. DUCOMMUN PROFESSOR OF EDUCATION AT STANFORD UNIVERSITY, WHERE SHE HAS LAUNCHED THE STANFORD EDUCATIONAL LEADERSHIP INSTITUTE AND THE SCHOOL REDESIGN NETWORK. SHE IS ALSO CO-FOUNDER OF A STANFORD-SPONSORED CHARTER SCHOOL THAT SERVES THE EAST PALO ALTO, CALIF., COMMUNITY AND HELPS TO TRAIN NEW

TEACHERS. AMONG HER MORE THAN 300 PUBLICATIONS IS *THE RIGHT TO LEARN*, RECIPIENT OF THE AMERICAN EDUCATIONAL RESEARCH ASSOCIATION'S OUTSTANDING BOOK AWARD FOR 1998, AND *TEACHING AS THE LEARNING PROFESSION* (CO-EDITED WITH GARY SYKES), RECIPIENT OF THE NATIONAL STAFF DEVELOPMENT COUNCIL'S OUTSTANDING BOOK AWARD FOR 2000.

KENNETH MONTGOMERY IS CURRENTLY A RESEARCH ANALYST FOR THE SCHOOL REDESIGN NETWORK AT STANFORD UNIVERSITY, WHERE HE IS ALSO A DOCTORAL STUDENT. MONTGOMERY HAS TAUGHT HIGH SCHOOL ENGLISH, SPEECH AND DEBATE, AND WORKED AS A MIDDLE SCHOOL ADMINISTRATOR. IN 2001, HE WAS CERTIFIED BY THE NATIONAL BOARD OF PROFESSIONAL TEACHING STANDARDS AND IN 2003 HE WAS RECOGNIZED BY *USA TODAY* AS ONE OF THE TOP TEACHERS IN THE NATION. HE ALSO HAS BEEN FEATURED ON A PBS SPECIAL AND IN A PROFESSIONAL DEVELOPMENT VIDEO ON METHODS FOR ENGAGING THE COMMUNITY IN THE CLASSROOM.

Endnotes

1. Scott, J. T. and Barber, M. E., "Charter Schools in California, Michigan, and Arizona: An Alternative Framework for Policy Analysis," *Occasional Paper* (New York: Teachers College, Columbia University, National Center for the Study of Privatization in Education, 2002) p. 39.
2. Hirschman, A., *Exit, Voice, and Loyalty Responses to Decline in Firms, Organizations, and States* (Cambridge: Harvard University Press, 1970).
3. Imberman, S., "Achievement and Behavior in Charter Schools: Drawing a More Complete Picture," *Occasional Paper No. 142* (New York: Teachers College, Columbia University, National Center for the Study of Privatization in Education, 2007) p. 48.
4. Miron, G. and Nelson, C., "Student Achievement in Charter Schools: What We Know and Why We Know So Little," *Occasional Paper No. 41* (New York: Teachers College, Columbia University, National Center for the Study of Privatization in Education, 2001) p. 36; American Federation of Teachers, *Do Charter Schools Measure Up? The Charter School Experiment After 10 Years* (Washington, D.C.: American Federation of Teachers, 2002).
5. Allen, J. and Mitchell, S., "Charter Schools: Changing the Face of American Education Today, Part 2: Raising the Bar on Charter School Laws, 2006 Ranking and Scorecard" (Washington, D.C.: The Center for Education Reform, 2006) p. 92.
6. Buckley, J. and Kuscova, S., "The Effects of Institutional Variation on Policy Outcomes: The Case of Charter Schools in the States," *Occasional Paper No. 79* (New York: Teachers College, Columbia University, National Center for the Study of Privatization in Education, 2003) p. 24.
7. Mead, S. and Rotherham, A. J., "A Sum Greater Than the Parts: What States Can Teach Each Other About Charter Schooling" (Washington D.C.: Education Sector, 2007).
8. Allen, J. and Mitchell, S., 2006, p. 92.

9. ibid.
10. Molnar, A., et al., "Profiles of For-profit Education Management Organizations" (Tempe, AZ: Commercialism in Education Research Unit, Education Policy Studies Laboratory, Arizona State University, 2007).
11. American Federation of Teachers (2002).
12. National School Boards Association Legal Clips, August 2006, www.nsba.org/site/doc_cosa.asp?TRACKID=&VID=50&CID=479&DID=39160.
13. See, for example, Vasquez Heilig, J. and Darling-Hammond, L., "Accountability Texas Style: The Progress and Learning of Urban Minority Students in a High-Stakes Testing Context," *Educational Evaluation and Policy Analysis* (2008, in press).
14. Miron, G., et al., "Evaluating the Impact of Charter Schools on Student Achievement: A Longitudinal Look at the Great Lakes States," Education Policy Research Unit, Arizona State University, and Education and the Public Interest Center, University of Colorado (2007), p. 20; Messina, I., "State to Review Charter School Concerns, 2005," retrieved from www.oh.aft.org/index.cfm?action=article&articleID=d2bd2915-42dd 487c-84ed-c311811bf95a on November 12, 2007.
15. Miron, et al., 2007.
16. Carnoy, M., et al., *The Charter School Dust-Up: Examining the Evidence on Enrollment and Achievement* (Washington, D.C.: Economic Policy Institute and Teachers College Press, 2005).
17. "California Charter Schools: Measuring Their Performance" (EdSource Online, 2007).
18. American Federation of Teachers, 2002; "Charter School Funding: Inequity's Next Frontier" (Washington, D.C.: Thomas B. Fordham Institute, 2005).
19. Mead, S. and Rotherham, A. J., 2007.
20. McGuinn, P., "The Policy Landscape of Educational Entrepreneurship," American Enterprise Institute Conference, Washington D.C., 2005.
21. Wells, A. S., *Beyond the Rhetoric of Charter School Reform: A Study of Ten California School Districts* (Los Angeles: UCLA, 1998); Bulkley, K. and Fisler, J., "A Decade of Charter Schools: From Theory to Practice," *Educational Policy* (2003), 17(3): 317-342.
22. Dingerson, L., "Unlovely: How the Market Is Failing the Children of New Orleans," *Keeping the Promise?* (Milwaukee: Rethinking Schools, 2008).
23. Wamba, N. G. and Ascher, C., "An Examination of Charter School Equity," *Education and Urban Society* (2003) 35(4): 462-476.
24. ibid.
25. Wells, 1998; Bulkley and Fisler, 2003; Mead and Rotherham, 2007.
26. Dodenhoff, D., "Fixing the Milwaukee Public Schools: The Limit of Parent-Driven Reforms," (Milwaukee: Wisconsin Policy Research Institute, 2007) p.15.
27. ibid.
28. Wamba and Ascher, 2003.
29. ibid.
30. Frankenberg, E. and Lee, C., "Charter Schools and Race: A Lost Opportunity for Integrated Education" (Cambridge: The Civil Rights Project at Harvard University, 2003).

31. Fuller (2001) in Buckley, J. and. Schneider, M., "Do Charter Schools Promote Student Citizenship," *Occasional Paper No. 91* (New York: Teachers College, Columbia University, National Center for the Study of Privatization in Education, 2004) p. 41.

32. McGuinn, 2005.

33. Becker, H., "School Board Reconsiders Mandarin Immersion," *The Paly Voice*, April 18, 2007, retrieved from voice.paly.net/view_story.php?id=5274, on February 5, 2008.

34. Wells, A.S., 1998; Bulkley and Fisler, 2003.

35. Bulkley and Fisler, 2003.

36. See for example, Sergiovanni, T., *Building Communities in Schools* (San Francisco: Jossey-Bass, 1994); Wasley, P., et al., *Small Schools: Great Strides; A Study of New Small Schools in Chicago* (New York: Bank Street College of Education, 2000); Darling-Hammond, L., Ancess, J., and Ort, S., "Reinventing High School: Outcomes of the Coalition Campus Schools Project," *American Educational Research Journal 39*, no. 3 (2002): 639–673; Fine, M., ed., *Charting Urban School Reform: Reflections on Public High Schools in the Midst of Change* (New York: Teachers College Press, 1994); Fine, M., Stoudt, B., and Futch, V., *The Internationals Network for Public Schools: A Quantitative and Qualitative Cohort Analysis of Graduation and Dropout Rates* (City University of New York, Graduate Center, 2005).

The Editors

Leigh Dingerson is the Education Team Leader at the Center for Community Change in Washington, D.C., where she has worked for a decade. She is the author of the center's October 2006 booklet on the New Orleans schools, *Dismantling a Community*, and is editor of the center's *Education Organizing* newsletter, which shares efforts of grassroots organizations working to improve public schools. She has also been a community organizer with ACORN, working in Texas, Arkansas, and South Carolina.

Barbara Miner has more than 30 years' experience as a writer, columnist, and editor for newspapers, magazines, and books. A former managing editor and continuing columnist for *Rethinking Schools* magazine, she writes often on education and other social issues. Her writings have appeared in publications from the *New York Times* to the *Nation*, the *Progressive*, *ColorLines*, *Milwaukee Magazine*, and the *Milwaukee Journal Sentinel*.

Bob Peterson is a teacher, writer, and organizer. He teaches 5th grade at La Escuela Fratney, a two-way bilingual public school in Milwaukee that he helped found. He is also a founding and current editor of *Rethinking Schools*, and serves on the executive board of the Milwaukee Teachers' Education Association. He has co-edited several books including *Transforming Teacher Unions: Fighting for Better Schools and Social Justice*; *Rethinking Mathematics: Teaching Social Justice by the Numbers*; and *Rethinking Globalization: Teaching for Justice in an Unjust World*.

Stephanie Walters is a longtime political and education activist in Milwaukee. She is an elementary teacher in the Milwaukee Public Schools (MPS), and has also held local and state leadership positions in the teacher union. She is currently on leave from her classroom duties in MPS and works as a staff person for the Milwaukee Teachers' Education Association, where she handles contract enforcement and professional development for new teachers in the district.

Collaborating Organizations

The Center for Community Change seeks to build the power and capacity of low-income people, particularly people of color, to change institutions and policies that affect their lives. Founded in 1968, the center strengthens community-based organizations and helps them unite across lines of race, geography, and issue in order to confront the vital issues of today and build the social movements of tomorrow. The Center's Education Team provides support to community organizations working to improve their public schools through greater parent engagement and policy reform. Website: www.communitychange.org.

Rethinking Schools, Ltd., is a nonprofit publisher advocating the reform of public schools. It stresses a commitment to social justice, with a particular focus on issues of race and urban schools. Founded in 1986 by classroom teachers, Rethinking Schools promotes a grassroots, activist perspective that combines theory and practice and links classroom issues to broader social concerns. In addition to book publishing, Rethinking Schools, Ltd., consists of a quarterly magazine, *Rethinking Schools*, and Rethinking Schools Online: www.rethinkingschools.org.

The Open Society Institute (OSI) is a private operating and grantmaking foundation that works to build vibrant and tolerant democracies whose governments are accountable to their citizens. To achieve its mission, OSI seeks to shape public policies that assure greater fairness in political, legal, and economic systems and safeguard fundamental rights. It supports people and organizations that advance a more open society within the United States and around the world. OSI places a high priority on protecting and improving the lives of marginalized people and communities. In the United States, OSI envisions a society that allows all people to participate actively and equitably in political, economic, and cultural life; encourages diverse opinions and critical debate on public issues; protects fundamental human rights, dignity, and the rule of law; and promotes broadly shared prosperity and human security. Website: www.soros.org.

Index

Resources from Rethinking Schools

Rethinking Schools Magazine

Rethinking Schools is a quarterly magazine written by teachers, parents, and education activists—people who understand the daily realities of reforming our schools. No other publication so successfully combines theory and practice while linking classroom issues to broader policy concerns.

> Three years: $39.95 (Save $19.45)
> Two years: $29.95 (Save $9.95)
> One year: $17.95
>
> Subscriptions to Canada and Mexico add $5 per year.
> Other international subscriptions add $10 per year.

Rethinking School Reform:
Views from the Classroom

A primer on a broad range of reform issues and how they promote— or prevent—the kind of teaching our schools and children need.

> Paperback • 350 pages • ISBN 0-942961-29-3 • $16.95

Transforming Teacher Unions:
Fighting for Better Schools and Social Justice

This anthology weaves together issues of critical importance to teacher unionism, with a special focus on issues of teacher professionalism and social justice in the classroom and in the community.

> Paperback • 144 pages • ISBN 0-942961-24-2 • $12.95

The Line Between Us:
Teaching About the Border and Mexican Immigration

Using stories, historical narrative, role plays, and videos, veteran teacher Bill Bigelow shows how he approaches immigration and border issues in his classroom.

> Paperback • 160 pages • ISBN: 978-0-942961-31-7 • $16.95

Rethinking Our Classrooms, Volume 1:
Teaching for Equity and Justice

Teaching ideas, compelling narratives, and hands-on examples of ways teachers can promote values of community, justice, and equality—and build academic skills.

> Paperback • 240 pages • ISBN 978-0-942961-35-5 • $16.95

Rethinking Globalization:
Teaching for Justice in an Unjust World

"A treasury of ideas and information," according to historian Howard Zinn. This comprehensive collection for teachers and activists includes role plays, interviews, poetry, stories, background readings, and hands-on teaching tools.

Paperback • 400 pages • ISBN 978-0-942961-31-7 • $18.95

Rethinking Mathematics:
Teaching Social Justice by the Numbers

Shows how to weave social justice issues throughout the mathematics curriculum, and how to integrate mathematics into other curricular areas.

Paperback • 180 pages • ISBN 978-0-942961-54-6 • $16.95

Open Minds to Equality:
A Sourcebook of Learning Activities to Affirm Diversity and Promote Equality

An educator's sourcebook of activities to help students understand and change inequalities based on race, gender, class, age, language, sexual orientation, and religion.

Paperback • 408 pages • ISBN: 978-0-942961-32-4 • $24.95

Reading, Writing, and Rising Up:
Teaching About Social Justice and the Power of the Written Word

Essays, lesson plans, and a remarkable collection of student writing, with an unwavering focus on language arts teaching for justice.

Paperback • 196 pages • ISBN 978-0-942961-25-6 • $12.95

FOUR EASY WAYS TO ORDER

Order online: www.rethinkingschools.org
Call toll-free: 800-669-4192
Fax: 802-864-7626
Mail: Rethinking Schools, PO Box 2222, Williston, VT 05495

MasterCard, Visa, and purchase orders accepted.

Call 800-669-4192 for a free catalog of materials
or visit www.rethinkingschools.org.